Learn Every Day About Bugs and Spiders

Edited by Kathy Charner

© 2010 Gryphon House, Inc.
Published by Gryphon House, Inc.
10770 Columbia Pike, Suite 201
Silver Spring, MD 20901
800.638.0928; 301.595.9500; 301.595.0051 (fax)

Visit us on the web at www.gryphonhouse.com

Illustrations: Deb Johnson

Library of Congress Cataloging-in-Publication Information:
Learn every day about bugs and spiders / edited by Kathy Charner.
      p. cm.
 ISBN 978-0-87659-128-4
1. Insects—Juvenile literature. 2. Spiders—Juvenile literature. I.
Charner, Kathy.
 QL467.2.L42 2010
 595.7—dc22

                                2009051772

BULK PURCHASE

Gryphon House books are available for special premiums and sales promotions as well as for fund-raising use. Special editions or book excerpts also can be created to specification. For details, contact the Director of Marketing at Gryphon House.

DISCLAIMER

Gryphon House, Inc. and the authors cannot be held responsible for damage, mishap, or injury incurred during the use of or because of activities in this book. Appropriate and reasonable caution and adult supervision of children involved in activities and corresponding to the age and capability of each child involved is recommended at all times. Do not leave children unattended at any time. Observe safety and caution at all times.

Table of Contents

Introduction 7

ART ACTIVITIES

3+
Stained-Glass Butterflies 9

4+
Bug Bodies....................................10
Spider Webs 11
Sticks-and-Stones Ants 12

BOOK ACTIVITIES

3+
Colorful Caterpillars 13
Ten Little Butterflies......................14
What's in the Grass?....................15

4+
Bug Safari 16
The Butterfly Counting Book 17
Butterfly Wings 18
Circle Caterpillars.........................19
Classic Carle 20
Dragonfly....................................21
The Grasshopper and the Ant........22
The Hungry Caterpillar...................23
Life Cycle of a Ladybug.................24
Mixing Colors...............................25
Spider Webs 26
What Rhymes with Ant?.................27

5+
Firefly Art 28
Praying Mantis 29

CIRCLE OR GROUP TIME ACTIVITIES

4+
Mayflies Flying Through
    the Week 30
Peek-a-Boo Good Morning.............31
Smell Flowers Like a Bee................32
Spiders..33
The Web of Life 34
What Is Your Favorite Insect?.........35

GAME ACTIVITIES

3+
Flutter-Hop Game........................36

4+
Birthday Bug Bags 37
Bugs on the Rug...........................38
Buzzin' Bees 39
Capture a Bug.............................40
Catch a Fly.................................41
Meet My Flying Friend 42
Crickets and Grasshoppers 43
Fireflies 44
Fly Like a Butterfly 45
Insect Cards 46
Insect Dominoes 47
Match the Insects 48
Mother, May I Move
    Like an Insect? 49
Smell Out Your Group! 50
Where's That Bug? 51

5+
Ladybug Counting Game...............52

LANGUAGE AND LITERACY ACTIVITIES

4+
Insect Name Matchup....................53
Jars 54
Literacy and Bees.........................55
Rhyming Caterpillars 56
Two Halves Make a Whole Bug......57
What Letter Sound Does
    Your Cricket Make? 58

5+
Bugs in Boxes..............................59
If I Were a Bug.............................60
Ladybug Letters............................61
Tracing Spider-Web Letters............62

LARGE MOTOR ACTIVITIES

3+
Ants in Your Pants! 63

4+
Bugs on the Balance Beam.............64
Flying Insects...............................65

MANIPULATIVES ACTIVITIES

3+
Butterfly Match 66
Taking Bees to the Flowers 67

MATH ACTIVITIES

3+
Butterfly Bonanza..........................68
Find the Bugs 69

4+
I Love Honey 70
Insect Shoe Patterns 71
Let Your Fingers Do the Sizing 72
Measuring with Caterpillars 73
Shape Bugs 74

5+
Bug Races 75
Counting Caterpillar Puzzle 76
Let's Count the Legs......................77
Six Legs...78

MUSIC AND MOVEMENT ACTIVITY

4+
Chirp, Cricket, Chirp!.....................79

OUTDOOR PLAY ACTIVITY

4+
Pollinators 80

REST AND NAP TIME ACTIVITIES

3+
Bottles of Bugs 81
Snuggle with a Bug........................82

SAND AND WATER PLAY ACTIVITY

4+
Bug Hunt.......................................83

SCIENCE AND NATURE ACTIVITIES

4+
Entomologist of the Day 84
Is It an Insect? 85

SMALL MOTOR ACTIVITIES

3+
Spider Webs 86

4+
Mason Bee Houses 87

SNACK AND COOKING ACTIVITIES

3+
Honey Milk Balls............................88

4+
Baking Ladybug Cookies 89
Butterfly Snack 90
Spider Web Snacks 91

SOCIAL DEVELOPMENT ACTIVITY

4+
The Good Deed Caterpillar............92

SONGS, POEMS, AND FINGERPLAY ACTIVITIES

3+
A Bumblebee Has Stripes...............93
How Insects Move 94
How Many Legs?............................95
Ladybug Poem 96
The Spider Song.............................97

4+
The Caterpillar Song......................98
Five Little Butterflies.......................99
From Caterpillar to Butterfly 100
I Can Be an Entomologist 101
A Spider Weaves..........................102
A Very Noisy Mosquito.................103
We're Going on a Bug Hunt........104
Which One Is It?..........................105

TRANSITION ACTIVITIES

3+
Follow the Ant 106

4+
Busy Beehive 107
Insect Pathway 108

INDEXES

Index of Children's Books..............109
Index 115

Note: The books listed in the Related Children's Books section of each activity may occasionally include books that are only available used or through your local library.

Introduction

You have in your hands a great teacher resource! This book, which is part of the *Learn Every Day* series, contains 100 activities you can use with children ages 3–6 to help them develop a lifelong love of learning, as well as the knowledge and skills all children need to become successful students in kindergarten and beyond. The activities in this book are written by teachers and professionals from the field of early childhood education—educators and professionals who use these activities in their classrooms every day.

The activities in the books are separated by curriculum areas, such as Art, Books, Outdoor Play, Transitions, and so on, and are organized according to their age appropriateness, so activities appropriate for children ages three and up come first, then activities appropriate for children age four and up, and finally, activities for children age five and up. Each activity has the following components—learning objectives, a list of related vocabulary words, a list of thematically related books, a list of the materials (if any) you need to complete the activity, directions for preparation and the activity itself. Also included in each activity is an assessment component to help you observe how well the children are meeting the learning objectives. Given the emphasis on accountability in early childhood education, these assessment strategies are essential.

Several activities also contain teacher-to-teacher tips that provide smart and useful ideas, including how to expand the central idea of an activity in a new way or where to find the materials necessary to complete a given activity. Some activities also include related fingerplays, poems, or songs that you can sing and chant with the children. Children love singing, dancing, and chanting, actions that help expand children's understanding of an activity's learning objectives.

This book, and the other books in this series, give early childhood educators 100 great activities that require few materials, little if any preparation, and are sure to make learning fun and engaging for children.

Stained-Glass Butterflies

3+

LEARNING OBJECTIVES

The children will:

1. Learn about colors and patterns in nature.
2. Practice their small motor skills.

Materials

cheese grater
broken crayons
cups
pictures of
    butterflies
wax paper
iron and ironing
    board
old towels

VOCABULARY

butterfly	different	pattern	sprinkle
color	meet	same	wings

PREPARATION

- Grate the broken crayons into small pieces, and place the pieces in cups on the table.
- Trace and cut butterfly shapes out of wax paper. Each child will need two.

WHAT TO DO

1. Show the children pictures of butterflies, and talk about how colorful their wings are. Be sure to point out how both wings look the same and share the same pattern.
2. Invite the children to create their own butterflies by sprinkling colorful crayon pieces on one of the wax paper butterflies.
3. When the children finish sprinkling crayon pieces on the wax paper butterflies, place the second butterfly on top of the first one, so that the crayon bits are sandwiched between the two layers.
4. Move the butterflies to a location away from the children for ironing.
5. Place a towel on a tabletop. Place another towel over the first butterfly and apply a warm iron. Move the iron around until all of the wax melts (Note: An adult-only step). The butterfly should now have a pretty stained-glass look.
6. Repeat with the remaining butterflies.
7. Hang the butterflies in a window for the children to enjoy.

Children's Books

Butterfly, Butterfly by
    Petr Horacek
*Velma Gratch and the
Way Cool Butterfly* by
    Alan Madison
*The Very Hungry
Caterpillar* by Eric Carle

ASSESSMENT

Consider the following:

- Ask the children if they know of other bugs that are colorful. Suggest ladybugs, bumblebees, and beetles if they get stuck.
- Have the children draw pictures of colorful make-believe bugs.

Erin Huffstetler, Maryville, TN

Bug Bodies

4+

LEARNING OBJECTIVES

The children will:

1. Learn that insects have three body sections and six legs.
2. Develop their small motor skills.

Materials

insect photos and
books
whiteboard and dry
erase marker
clay or playdough

VOCABULARY

abdomen	eyes	legs	stinger
antennae	head	mandible	thorax
body	jaws	shape	

WHAT TO DO

1. Show the children a picture of an insect and ask them to describe what they see.
2. Write the children's observations on a whiteboard. Point out the head, and discuss features such as eyes, mandibles, and antennae. Now, have the children focus on the thorax and teach that an insect's six legs grow out of the thorax.
3. Look at the insect's abdomen and let the children talk about what they see. They might notice hairs or special coloring on this part of the bug body. Teach that stingers are part of the abdomen. Has anyone ever been stung by a bee? Write all the new words on the board for the children to read.
4. Now, pass a bug book (see suggestions below) around the circle and have each child choose a picture.
5. Have the child point out the three body parts and other features. Note the wide variety of shapes in insect bodies; three body sections will still be visible.
6. Finally, show the children how to roll a small ball of clay to make an insect head, a medium ball for the thorax, and a larger ball for the abdomen.
7. Demonstrate how to roll six small cylinders for the legs, and assemble the bug body. Complete with antennae, eyes, and jaws.
8. Also consider using clay tools to press patterns into the body. Children might choose a particular type of insect to recreate in clay.

TEACHER-TO-TEACHER TIP

- Consider asking the children to point out the similarities and differences between human and insect bodies.

ASSESSMENT

Consider the following:

- Can the children say how many body sections and how many legs an insect has?
- Are the children able to make basic insect body shapes out of the clay?

Children's Books

The Bug Cemetery by
Frances Hill
I Like Bugs by
Margaret Wise Brown
*The Very Clumsy Click
Beetle* by Eric Carle

Patrick Mitchell, Yagoto, Nagoya, Japan

Spider Webs

4+

LEARNING OBJECTIVES

The children will:

1. Learn how spiders live, what they eat, how they help us, and that they spin webs.
2. Develop their small motor skills.

paper
pencil
black marker
wax paper
tape
glue
glitter

VOCABULARY

fragile	spider web	trace
spider	spin	

PREPARATION

- Before class, draw or copy a large spider web. Make sure that you go over the web with a black marker so the lines can be seen through wax paper.
- Make several copies of this web to use with the children in your class. This is a project that you may only want to have children work on two at a time so you can help supervise.

WHAT TO DO

1. Tape a copy of the spider web to the table.
2. Tear off a larger piece of wax paper to place over the copy of the spider web. Tape the wax paper to the table.
3. Ask the children to use glue to track the spider web that you copied earlier on to the wax paper. When they have completed tracing the web with glue, sprinkle glitter over top of the glue. Let dry completely.
4. Peel off the wax paper to reveal a beautiful glittering spider web that you can hang anywhere in the classroom or at home.
5. Ask the children to be very careful with these webs, because they are very fragile just like real spider webs.

Children's Books

Anansi Does the Impossible! An Ashanti Tale retold by Verna Aardema
Little Miss Spider by David Kirk
Miss Spider's Tea Party by David Kirk

ASSESSMENT

Consider the following:

- Do the children indicate an understanding that spiders live in webs?
- Are the children able to create and decorate their spider webs?

Cookie Zingarelli, Columbus, OH

Sticks-and-Stones Ants

4+

LEARNING OBJECTIVES

The children will:

1. Make ants from sticks and stones.
2. Learn about the body parts of ants.
3. Practice small motor skills.
4. Practice following directions.

images of ants
wax paper
tacky glue
small pebbles
short twigs

VOCABULARY

abdomen	body	head	legs
antennae	exoskeleton	insect	thorax

WHAT TO DO

1. Set out various images of ants for the children to look at. Discuss with the children the ants' characteristics.
2. Lay out wax paper on the table tops.
3. Demonstrate to the children how to glue the pebbles together to resemble the three sections of an ant's body.
4. Demonstrate how to glue on the six small twig legs and two small twig antennae.
5. As the children create their own ants of sticks and stones, discuss each of the body parts.

ASSESSMENT

Consider the following:

- Can the children tell you how many sections make up an ant's body?
- Ask the children to name the parts of the ant.
- Can the children tell you how many legs and antennae an ant has?

Kimberly Hutmacher, Illiopolis, IL

Children's Books

Are You an Ant? by Judy Allen and Tudor Humphries
Hey, Little Ant by Philip M. Hoose and Hannah Hoose
The Life and Times of the Ant by Charles Micucci

LEARN EVERY DAY ABOUT BUGS AND SPIDERS

Colorful Caterpillars

LEARNING OBJECTIVES

The children will:
1. Improve their color recognition skills.
2. Learn to compare objects by size and shape.

Materials

The Very Hungry Caterpillar by Eric Carle
30 or more colorful chenille stems
markers
pencils
green felt
scissors (adult use only)
1 or more plastic bug catchers

VOCABULARY

caterpillar	crawl	leaf
color	fuzzy	small

PREPARATION

- Make at least 30 caterpillars from chenille stems by wrapping a chenille stem around a marker to create a tight coil. Remove the marker for a fat caterpillar. For a skinnier caterpillar, wrap the chenille stem around a pencil.
- Cut four 8" × 10" leaves from green felt.
- Place the caterpillars and leaves in the plastic bug catcher(s).

WHAT TO DO

1. Read *The Very Hungry Caterpillar* by Eric Carle. Invite the children to explore a caterpillar manipulative as you read the story aloud.
2. Invite a child to open the bug catcher and remove a leaf.
3. Have the child spill out the caterpillars.
4. Invite the child to place each caterpillar on the large felt leaf and describe it.
5. Encourage the children to sort the caterpillars by color or size and then line them up in a row and count them.
6. Invite the children to move the caterpillars about the leaves as they work and play. Talk about how caterpillars move.
7. Encourage the children to invent conversations the caterpillars could have with one another as they move about the leaf.
8. Invite the older children to create a pattern using the caterpillar manipulatives and then teach the pattern to a friend.

ASSESSMENT

Consider the following:
- Can the children describe the butterflies?
- Are the children able to use props to retell the story of *The Very Hungry Caterpillar?*

Children's Books

Butterfly, Butterfly by Petr Horacek
Butterfly Express by Jane Belk Moncure
Flying Colors: Butterflies in Your Backyard by Nancy Loewen

Mary J. Murray, Mazomanie, WI

Ten Little Butterflies

3+

LEARNING OBJECTIVES

The children will:
1. Learn about the life cycle of butterflies.
2. Learn to count from 1–10.

Materials

books about butterflies (see list for suggestions)

VOCABULARY

butterfly   number words "one" through "ten"
fly   sky
little

WHAT TO DO

1. Gather the children in a circle. Read them one of the books about butterflies from the list below.
2. Talk with the children about the butterfly in the story. Ask them to describe the butterfly.
3. Sing the following song with the children, asking them to hold up the appropriate number of fingers as the song progresses:

Ten Little Butterflies by Shyamala Shanmugasundaram
(Tune: "Bumping Up and Down in My Little Red Wagon")
One little, two little, three little butterflies,
Four little, five little, six little butterflies,
Seven little, eight little, nine little butterflies,
Ten butterflies flying in the sky.

TEACHER-TO-TEACHER TIP

- Use face paint to make butterfly tattoos on every child's arm.

ASSESSMENT

Consider the following:
- Can the child point to a butterfly when shown assorted insect pictures?
- Is the child beginning to learn to count?

Children's Books

Are You a Butterfly? by Judy Allen and Tudor Humphries
Butterflies by Karen Shapiro
Butterfly by Susan Canizares
The Very Hungry Caterpillar by Eric Carle

Shyamala Shanmugasundaram, Nerul, Navi Mumbai, India

What's in the Grass?

LEARNING OBJECTIVES

The children will:
1. Practice their language and literacy skills.
2. Gain familiarity with creatures that live in the fields and grass.
3. Participate successfully in a movement activity depicting creatures from a storybook.

Materials

In the Tall, Tall Grass by Denise Fleming
art materials:
  construction paper, paper plates, yarn
markers
crayons
glue or paste
mural paper

VOCABULARY

act out	environment	meadow	mural
crawl	grass	move	tall

WHAT TO DO

1. Read the book *In the Tall, Tall Grass* by Denise Fleming to the children.
2. Pause to explain unfamiliar vocabulary.
3. Invite individual children to act out the action words in the book using their bodies.
4. Read the story again and ask the children to move as a group and act out the words in the story.
5. Create a Tall, Tall Grass mural with the children creating the animals and insects from the story from construction paper, paper plates, yarn, and other scrap materials.

TEACHER-TO-TEACHER TIP

● Pair this story with Fleming's *In the Small, Small Pond* or *Barnyard Banter* to enhance your study of animals.

ASSESSMENT

Consider the following:
● Do the children listen attentively to the story?
● Can the group participate actively and appropriately in the movement and story reading?
● Does everyone add to the mural?

Children's Books

Charlie the Caterpillar by Dom Deluise
In the Small, Small Pond by Denise Fleming
Ladybug, Ladybug, Where Are You? by Cyndy Szekeres

Margery Kranyik Fermino, West Roxbury, MA

Bug Safari

4+

LEARNING OBJECTIVES

The children will:
1. Learn to identify common bugs.
2. Make observations about bugs.

Materials

children's book about insects (see list below for suggestions)
black-and-white pictures of bugs
paper
pencils (1 per child)
crayons

VOCABULARY

bug	hop	insect	observe	safety
fly	identify	look	safari	

PREPARATION

- Prepare an observation sheet. Include black-and-white pictures and names of bugs common to your area.
- Separate the bugs into groups such as "flying bugs," "hopping bugs," and "crawling bugs."
- Provide blank areas on the observation sheet where the children can draw bugs they find that are not listed.

WHAT TO DO

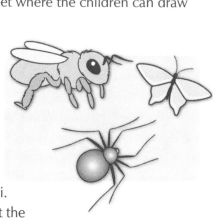

1. Read a book about bugs to the children (see list below for suggestions).
2. Discuss the characteristics of the bugs mentioned in the books.
3. Hand out observation sheets and pencils. Either hand out crayons or have them accessible for the children during their safari.
4. Discuss any safety rules and boundaries that the children must follow during the safari.
5. Take the children outside and let them explore.
6. Suggest that the children color the outline of the bugs on their observations sheets when they identify them.
7. When the safari is finished, have the class talk about the bugs they saw.

TEACHER-TO-TEACHER TIP

- To add a math element, give each child a ruler and have them include measurements for the bugs they find.

ASSESSMENT

Consider the following:
- Can the children identify common bugs?
- What did the children learn about bugs?

Children's Books

Ant, Ant, Ant: An Insect Chant by April Pulley Sayre
Bug Safari by Bob Barner
Have You Seen Bugs? by Joanne Oppenheim

Janet Hammond, Mount Laurel, NJ

The Butterfly Counting Book

LEARNING OBJECTIVES

The children will:
1. Practice their counting skills.
2. Develop their small motor skills.

The Butterfly Counting Book by Jerry Pallotta
paper cutouts of butterflies of varying sizes
crayons
drawing paper
scissors

VOCABULARY

butterfly	count	numeral names	size
cocoon	moth	outline	trace

PREPARATION

* Look online for sample outlines of butterflies to use in this activity.

WHAT TO DO

1. Read *The Butterfly Counting Book* by Jerry Pallotta to the children.
2. Have the children help you count the butterflies on each page.
3. Look at the different butterflies and see if you can find them in other pictures or books.

4. After reading the book, talk with the children about butterflies. Specifically, discuss how caterpillars turn into butterflies.
5. Set out several butterfly outlines, paper, and crayons.
6. Invite the children to make butterfly counting pages of their own by sketching the outlines of different butterfly cutouts.
7. Challenge the children to count the number of butterfly outlines they make on their papers.

Children's Books

Butterfly by Susan Canizares
Butterflies by Karen Shapiro
The Very Hungry Caterpillar by Eric Carle

ASSESSMENT

Consider the following:
* How well do the children count the butterflies in the book?
* Can the children trace the outlines of the butterfly cutouts?
* How well do the children count their own butterflies?

Cookie Zingarelli, Columbus, OH

Butterfly Wings

4+

LEARNING OBJECTIVES

The children will
1. Develop their small motor skills.
2. Learn about butterflies.

Materials

The Very Hungry Caterpillar by Eric Carle
poster board
string
scissors (adult use only)
crayons
markers
glitter
glue
headbands
pipe cleaners
pompoms or Styrofoam balls

VOCABULARY

antennae	caterpillar	wings
butterfly	fly	

PREPARATION

- Make a set of butterfly wings out of poster board for each child in the class.
- Attach string to make straps so that the children can put them on themselves.

WHAT TO DO

1. Read *The Very Hungry Caterpillar* by Eric Carle to the children. Afterwards, engage the children in a discussion about caterpillars.
2. Set out the materials and explain to the children that they will be making butterfly wings.
3. Have the children decorate the wings with crayons, markers, and glitter.
4. Attach the pipe cleaners to the headbands to make antennae. You can use small pompoms or small Styrofoam balls at the end of the antennae.
5. Let your little "butterflies" fly around the classroom or do a butterfly dance. Let them pretend to fly from flower to flower.
6. The children can also act out the story of *The Very Hungry Caterpillar*. It's a great way to have fun.

ASSESSMENT

Consider the following:
- Are the children able to decorate their butterfly wings?
- Are the children able to act out the story of *The Very Hungry Caterpillar*?

Cookie Zingarelli, Columbus, OH

Children's Books

Butterflies by Karen Shapiro
Butterflies! by Darlene Freeman
Why Butterflies Go by on Silent Wings by Marguerite W. David

Circle Caterpillars

4+

LEARNING OBJECTIVES

The children will:

1. Follow directions to create caterpillar art using circles.
2. Develop their small motor skills.

Materials

The Very Hungry Caterpillar by Eric Carle
green and red colored paper
one sheet of white background paper for each child
glue
crayons or markers

VOCABULARY

body	circle	head	pigment
butterfly	color names	hump	red
caterpillar	green	part	straight line

PREPARATION

- Cut out equal sized circles from green and red paper. There should be four or five green circles and one red circle for each child.
- On the background paper, write "My caterpillar has ___ circles."

WHAT TO DO

1. Read *The Very Hungry Caterpillar* by Eric Carle to the children. Look at the caterpillar illustrations and discuss how caterpillars are made up of many segments.
2. Hand out the circles and the background paper.
3. Have the children glue the circles together to make caterpillars with green bodies and red heads. Let the children decide if the caterpillar's circles run in a straight line or form a hump.
4. Have the children use markers or crayons to draw faces on their caterpillars.
5. Instruct the children to count the circles and then help the children write in the number of circles that make up their caterpillars.

TEACHER-TO-TEACHER TIP

- You can decide how many circles each child gets or you can let the children choose the number they want.

Children's Books

The Caterpillar and the Polliwog by Jack Kent
Charlie the Caterpillar by Dom Deluise
Clara Caterpillar by Pamela Duncan Edwards

ASSESSMENT

Consider the following:

- Can the child place the circles together to make them look like a caterpillar?
- Can the child correctly identify how many circles were used to make the caterpillar?

Janet Hammond, Mount Laurel, NJ

Classic Carle

4+

LEARNING OBJECTIVES

The children will:

1. Learn about a popular author/illustrator of picture books (Eric Carle).
2. Learn that Eric Carle liked to write stories about insects.
3. Express themselves by creating collages similar to Eric Carle's illustrations.

Materials

3 or more Eric Carle books (see list of children's books)
paper
paste or glue
child-safe scissors
colorful magazine pages

VOCABULARY

author	Eric Carle	specific insect names
collage	illustrator	
different	same	

PREPARATION

- Place the books on display in the reading area.
- Set materials for making collages in the art area.

WHAT TO DO

1. Show the books to the children during circle or group time. Explain that an author named Eric Carle liked to write stories about insects. Ask the children to identify "same" and "different" qualities among the books.
2. Talk with the children about the different insects that appear in each of Carle's books. Ask the children to describe the physical characteristics of each insect.
3. Explain to the children that Eric Carle made pictures for his stories by cutting and pasting colorful papers together. This type of artwork is called a "collage."
4. Read a different title each day.
5. Direct the children to move to the art area after they hear the story to design their own collages.

ASSESSMENT

Consider the following:

- Do the children understand that all of Eric Carle's books were written by a single author?
- Can the children name one or more of the bugs that Eric Carle writes about?

Susan Sharkey, Fletcher Hills, CA

Children's Books

The Grouchy Ladybug by Eric Carle
The Honeybee and the Robber by Eric Carle
The Very Busy Spider by Eric Carle
The Very Clumsy Click Beetle by Eric Carle
The Very Hungry Caterpillar by Eric Carle
The Very Lonely Firefly by Eric Carle
The Very Quiet Cricket by Eric Carle

Dragonfly

4+

LEARNING OBJECTIVES

The children will:

1. Develop observation skills.
2. Learn about dragonflies.
3. Develop respect for the environment.
4. Develop a foundation for later learning in biology.
5. Understand the difference between a dragonfly and a butterfly.

Materials

pictures of
dragonflies,
butterflies, and
other insects
paper
colored pencils or
crayons

VOCABULARY

butterfly	dragonfly	insect	pond
different	environment	mosquito	same

PREPARATION

- Have any of the teachers or parents taken photographs of dragonflies? If so, have them bring these to class.

WHAT TO DO

1. Read one or more of the dragonfly books and discuss the books with the children. Have any of them seen a dragonfly?
2. Talk about where we see these insects—near ponds and other bodies of water. They are insects and have six legs but they can't walk. Discuss this with the children.
3. Talk about the differences between a dragonfly and a butterfly.
4. Talk about how dragonflies help us by eating mosquitoes. What should we do when we see a dragonfly? (Don't try to touch. Just observe.)
5. Show the pictures of various insects to the children. Have them pick out the pictures of dragonflies.
6. Encourage the children to draw pictures of dragonflies.

ASSESSMENT

Consider the following:

- Can the children identify dragonflies?
- Can the children tell which pictures are other insects? (They don't need to identify the other insects.) What else can they tell you about dragonflies?

Children's Books

Are You a Dragonfly? by
Judy Allen and
Tudor Humphries
*Dazzling Dragonflies: A
Life Cycle Story* by
Linda Glaser
*The Dragonfly Next
Door* by John Adams
The Dragonfly Pool by
Eva Ibbotson
Dragonfly's Tale by
Kristina Rodanas

Shirley Anne Ramaley, Sun City, AZ

The Grasshopper and the Ant

4+

LEARNING OBJECTIVES

The children will:
1. Practice effective listening and comprehension skills.
2. Learn to recall specific details about a story.

Materials

Aesop's Fables
(many versions
are available,
including one by
Anna Milbourne)

VOCABULARY

Aesop	fable	lazy	work
ant	grasshopper	moral	

PREPARATION

● Review the story so you can read or tell it in a dramatic manner.

WHAT TO DO

1. Explain to the children that a fable is a special kind of story that teaches us a lesson about life. The lesson is called a moral. A moral reminds us to make smart choices.
2. Tell the children you will be reading them a story about a grasshopper and an ant. Explain that this fable comes from a very wise man named Aesop who lived in the country of Greece many, many years ago. His fables are so wonderful that children like you are still learning his lessons today.
3. Explain that the moral of the fable is: "There's a time to work and a time to play."
4. Read or tell the fable to the children. As you read, talk about grasshoppers and ants, and what they do: talk about how ants are known to work hard all the time to build and maintain their anthills. Grasshoppers don't build nests, but they live in grassy areas and jump from plant to plant.
5. Use the assessment questions below to review the fable with the children.

ASSESSMENT

Consider the following:
● Ask the children some questions about "The Grasshopper and the Ant":

  ● Who worked hard in the summer to collect food?
  ● Who danced and played all summer long?
  ● Who had plenty of food to eat when winter came?
  ● Who felt hungry that winter?
  ● Do you know the name of the wise man who told this story long ago?
  ● Can you remember the moral of this story?

Susan Sharkey, Fletcher Hills, CA

Children's Books

Are You a Grasshopper?
by Judy Allen
*Crickets and
Grasshoppers* by
Ann O. Squire
*Discovering Crickets
and Grasshoppers* by
Keith Porter

The Hungry Caterpillar

4+

LEARNING OBJECTIVES

The children will:
1. Learn about caterpillars.
2. Memorize a song.
3. Develop their small motor skills.

Materials

book on caterpillars
(see list below)
leaves (optional)
green and brown
construction
paper
markers and
crayons
child-safe scissors

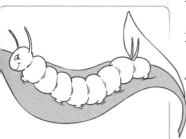

Children's Books

Clara Caterpillar by
Pamela Duncan
Edwards
*From Caterpillar
to Butterfly* by
Deborah Heiligman
*The Crunching
Munching Caterpillar* by
Sheridan Cain
*The Very Hungry
Caterpillar* by Eric Carle

VOCABULARY

butterfly   caterpillar   chrysalis   cut out   leaf   trace

PREPARATION

- Ahead of time, cut out a caterpillar from construction paper and laminate. If you don't have real leaves, cut out and laminate paper leaves.

WHAT TO DO

1. Read books about caterpillars (see the list of suggestions below) to the children.
2. Set out the various materials. Show the children how to trace a leaf on green paper, and then help the children cut them out.
3. Help the children trace the caterpillar outline on brown paper, and cut it out as well.
4. Recite the following fingerplay with the children:

The Hungry Caterpillar by Kristen Peters
(Tune "The Eensy, Weensy Spider")

The very hungry caterpillar
    (rub tummy)
Munched upon a leaf.
    (open and close hand like
    a duck quacking)
She made a cozy chrysalis
    (fold hands together)

To give herself relief.
She slept for many days
Growing as time went by.
When she awoke
She became a butterfly!
    (unfold hands keeping thumbs
    crossed, flap hands)

5. Invite the children to repeat the song, acting out the lines using their cutout caterpillars and leaves.

ASSESSMENT

Consider the following:
- Are the children able to recite the fingerplay?
- How well do the children cut out their leaves and caterpillars?

Kristen Peters, Mattituck, NY

Life Cycle of a Ladybug

LEARNING OBJECTIVES

The children will:
1. Learn where ladybugs live.
2. Learn the stages in development of a ladybug.

Materials

5 pictures depicting
the stages in
development of
a ladybug from
egg to adult
tagboard
glue stick
child-safe scissors
computer or
marker
laminator (optional)
binding machine
and plastic spine
(optional)

VOCABULARY

aphid	eggs	ladybug	pupa
develop	hatch	larva	stage

PREPARATION

- Create a book showing the development of a ladybug. Illustrate and write captions for each stage of development. Laminate and bind the pages inside the covers.

Eggs

Larva

Pupa

Adult

WHAT TO DO

1. Engage the children in a discussion about ladybugs. Ask the children what they look like.
2. Show the children the book (see Preparation).
3. Read the book aloud and put it in the reading area for further use.

TEACHER-TO-TEACHER TIP

- You may be able to find pictures in an old science book or magazine.

ASSESSMENT

Consider the following:
- Show the children images of the different stages in the ladybug's life cycle and ask them to put them in the correct order.
- Can the children name some of the different life stages of the ladybug?

Children's Books

Are You a Ladybug? by
Judy Allen
The Grouchy Ladybug
by Eric Carle
A Ladybug's Life by
John Himmelman
Ten Little Ladybugs by
Melanie Gerth and
Laura Huliska-Beith

Jackie Wright, Enid, OK

Mixing Colors

4+

LEARNING OBJECTIVES

The children will:
1. Mix two colors with their "clumsy beetle" to make a new color.
2. Develop their small motor skills.

Materials

The Very Clumsy Click Beetle by Eric Carle
tan or yellow oval sponges
black permanent marker
finger paint (red, blue, yellow, green, white, black)
wax paper
index cards

VOCABULARY

blend	bug	color names	shell
body	click beetle	mix	

PREPARATION

- Read books about beetles.
- Pour the following pairs of paint colors on separate pieces of wax paper:
  - blue and yellow
  - yellow and red
  - red and green
  - red and white
  - red and blue
  - white and black
- Use a black permanent marker to draw eyes on the sponges to make several "clumsy beetles" for each color pair station.

WHAT TO DO

1. Read *The Very Clumsy Click Beetle* by Eric Carle to the children.
2. Discuss the story with the children. Talk with the children about the beetle, and discuss what makes a beetle an insect. Ask the children to identify its various body parts.
3. Put the children into groups at each color station. Give each child six index cards.
4. Explain that the children can crawl the "clumsy beetles" from one color paint on the wax paper into the other, then make a print on the index card. What color did the beetle make?
5. Groups can move from station to station to try different color pairs.

SONG

I'm a Little Beetle by Kristen Peters   (Tune: "I'm a Little Teapot")

I'm a little beetle,   *I have a tiny body,*
My shell is hard.   *It's hard to see.*
I'm on a leaf   *So watch your step*
Or somewhere in your yard. *Or you'll step on me!*

ASSESSMENT

Consider the following:
- Can the children predict what will happen when they mix two colors together?
- Are the children able to move their beetles through the paint?

Kristen Peters, Mattituck, NY

Children's Books

Beetle Bop by Denise Fleming
Beetles by Edana Eckart
Bug Safari by Bob Barner
Have You Seen Bugs? by Joanne Oppenheim

Spider Webs

4+

LEARNING OBJECTIVES

The children will:
1. Improve their small motor skills.
2. Learn that spiders have eight legs.
3. Learn about the making of a web.
4. Learn about the use of webs.
5. Understand that spider webs come in many shapes and sizes.

Materials

The Very Busy Spider by Eric Carle
large piece of construction paper (white or light blue)
empty copy paper box top
tongs
golf ball
black tempera paint
spider stamps
washable black or brown stamp pads

VOCABULARY

ink	press	spider web	spinnerets
pad	spider	spiderling	stamp

WHAT TO DO

1. Read *The Very Busy Spider* by Eric Carle to the children.
2. Talk with the children about spider webs. Ask the children what spiders do with their webs, and why they make them where they do.
3. Discuss the making of a spider web. Ask each child to press the spider stamp into the ink pad then press the stamp onto the paper provided.
4. Place the paper with the spider stamps on it into the empty copy paper box top.
5. Use tongs to gently drop a golf ball into a tray of black paint.
6. Transfer the golf ball onto the paper with the spider stamps and slowly and cautiously roll the ball onto the paper rocking the box top back and forth while the golf ball creates web markings across the paper.
7. Let the paint dry. Display the spider and spider webs.

SONG

- Seat the children in a circle (this will be the "web").
- Ask one child to walk around the web as the group sings the song below.
- Pause to allow another child to be selected to join the first child and insert that child's name in the song!

Spider Song (Traditional)

One black spider went out to play
On a spider web one day.
He had such enormous fun,

He asked one more spider to come.
Spider (child's name) come out to play.
Spider (child's name) come out to play.

ASSESSMENT

Consider the following:

- Observe each child's small motor skills.
- Ask specific questions about the spider: How many legs does a spider have? What does the spider use a web for? What is an important role for the spider? How many parts are there in the spider's body?

Kaethe Lewandowski, Centreville, VA

Children's Books

Anansi Does the Impossible! An Ashanti Tale retold by Verna Aardema
Little Miss Spider by David Kirk
Miss Spider's Tea Party by David Kirk

What Rhymes with Ant?

4+

LEARNING OBJECTIVES

The children will:
1. Model the use of rhyming words as in this story.
2. Identify the rhyming words.

Materials

"I Can't," Said the Ant by Polly Cameron
images of ants or an ant farm (optional)
chart paper
marker

VOCABULARY

ant   character   rhyme   spout   story   stout   teapot

PREPARATION

● Have area clear for a group reading of the book.
● Set up easel with chart paper and marker readily available.

WHAT TO DO

Note: This should be a two-day activity.
1. On the first day, begin by discussing ants with the children. Talk with the children about how ants live in colonies, and describe their various characteristics. Consider showing the children some pictures of ants, or setting out an ant farm.
2. Read *"I Can't," Said the Ant* by Polly Cameron to the whole class.
3. After reading the book, discuss the setting, problem, and solution of the story with the children. Dismiss the children by asking them to name a character from the story.
4. On the second day, gather the group to discuss the hunt for rhyming words from the story.
5. Review the story and explain that you will only be reading small bits.
6. Tell the children that when they hear two rhyming words, they should raise their hands. List each pair of words on the chart paper.
7. After filling the chart paper, dismiss the children by asking them to think of two rhyming words of their own. Help those who have not grasped the concept.
8. Afterwards, hang the chart paper on the wall to display the group's work.

TEACHER-TO-TEACHER TIP

● This may be a new concept to some. Coach those who have difficulty. Follow up individually if further practice is needed.

ASSESSMENT

Consider the following:
● Can the children describe the story in *"I Can't," Said the Ant*?
● Can the children name some words that rhyme with "ant"?

Children's Books

Are You an Ant? by Judy Allen and Tudor Humphries
Hey, Little Ant by Philip M. Hoose and Hannah Hoose
The Life and Times of the Ant by Charles Micucci

Terry Troy, Tolland, CT

Firefly Art

5+

LEARNING OBJECTIVES

The children will:

1. Learn that fireflies (also called lightning bugs) emit a glow that can be seen in the dark.
2. Make firefly drawings from dots that will light up in the dark.

Materials

black construction paper
fluorescent paint
small paintbrush
white colored pencils
blacklight (optional)

VOCABULARY

dark	glow	lightning	night
firefly	light	locate	

PREPARATION

- Make five dots with fluorescent paint on a sheet of paper. Place a dot 2″ from each corner and one in the center. Make one sheet for each child.
- Allow the paint to dry. Make sure the paint is exposed to enough light to glow at the end of the activity. **Note:** Consider using a blacklight to highlight the fluorescence in the paint.
- Drape some dark fabric over a table to create a dark space to be used to view results.

WHAT TO DO

1. Read one of the firefly stories suggested below. Explain that these insects (also known as "lightning bugs") flash their lights to locate one another in the dark.
2. Pass out the papers and pencils. Ask the children to find each of the five dots and turn them into fireflies. To do so, they might draw a narrow loop above each dot for the body, a circle at the top of the body for the head, and two additional loops on each side of the body to form the wings.
3. Encourage the children to take turns crawling under the table with their drawings to see their firefly lights glow in the dark.

Children's Books

Fireflies by Megan E. Bryant
Fireflies in the Night by Judy Hawes
Sam and the Firefly by P. D. Eastman
Ten Flashing Fireflies by Philemon Sturges

ASSESSMENT

Consider the following:

- Can the children say how fireflies differ from other insects?
- Are the children engaged while making their firefly drawings?

Susan Sharkey, Fletcher Hills, CA

Praying Mantis

5+

LEARNING OBJECTIVES

The children will:
1. Learn about the praying mantis and what it eats.
2. Understand that the mantis is not poisonous, but we should leave insects alone.
3. Increase their vocabulary and language skills.

Materials

book about the praying mantis (see list for suggestions)
paper
writing pencils, colored pencils and/or crayons

VOCABULARY

bugs	native	prey
insects	praying mantis	

PREPARATION
- Place materials on the tables.
- Write the words "praying mantis" in large letters on a sheet of paper. Place it where the children can see it.

WHAT TO DO
1. Sitting in a circle, talk about the praying mantis with the children. Ask them why they think it's called a "praying" mantis.
2. Read one of the books about praying mantises and show them pictures of this insect.
3. Tell the children the mantis is not poisonous but we should leave them, and all bugs, alone. Farmers often use the praying mantis to control other insects, so it is helpful to keep praying mantises safe for farmers' crops.
4. As the children sit at tables, challenge them to draw a praying mantis, and if appropriate, to write "praying mantis" on their drawings.

Children's Books

Manuelo, the Playing Mantis by Don Freeman
Praying Mantises by Jason Cooper
Praying Mantises by Colleen A. Sexton
Praying Mantises: Hungry Insect Heroes by Sandra Markle

TEACHER-TO-TEACHER TIP
- There are many websites that offer free clip art images of praying mantises.

ASSESSMENT
Consider the following:
- Ask the children to talk about the praying mantis.
- Can the children explain why farmers like these insects?
- Can the children explain why we shouldn't touch these insects, or any bugs? (Some might bite, some might be poisonous, and we should not disturb the creature's lives.)

Shirley Anne Ramaley, Sun City, AZ

Mayflies Flying Through the Week

4+

LEARNING OBJECTIVES

The children will:

1. Identify left-to-right movement.
2. Name the days of the week.
3. Enhance their understanding of the calendar.

Materials

images of flies and mayflies
index cards
markers

VOCABULARY

calendar	different	flyswatter	same
days of the week	fly	mayflies	swat

PREPARATION

- Find and set out images of various flies and mayflies.
- Write the days of the week on index cards. Display the word cards across the top of the calendar area bulletin board, within reach of the children.

WHAT TO DO

1. Talk with the children about flies. Ask the children to talk about times that they have seen flies. Explain that there are flies and there are mayflies. Show the children images of each. Explain that one of the major differences between the two types of flies is that mayflies usually live for only one day, while other flies can live for a few weeks.
2. Show the children images of flies and other insects, and challenge the children to identify the flies.
3. Each morning, give one child an image of a mayfly, and ask the child to tape the image below the word card that has the current day's name on it.
4. Encourage the rest of the children in the class to help the child.
5. Say the name of the day with the children together, and ask the children to say the names of the days that come before and after that day.

ASSESSMENT

Consider the following:

- Can the children say what day it is?
- Can the children distinguish a fly from other insects?

Mary J. Murray, Mazomanie, WI

Children's Books

Hi, Fly Guy by Tedd Arnold
On Beyond Bugs: All About Insects by Tish Rabe
The Very Quiet Cricket by Eric Carle

Peek-a-Boo Good Morning 4+

LEARNING OBJECTIVES

The children will:
1. Say "good morning" to a selection of insects.
2. Identify various insects based on physical characteristics.
3. Develop their social skills.

Materials

plastic drinking
  cups (16 oz.)
small plastic toy
  insects and paper
  cutouts of insects
wooden dowel or
  paint stirring stick
glue
insect stickers

VOCABULARY

good morning	insects	see
hello	peek	smile

PREPARATION

- Display an assortment of plastic cups upside down around the border of one or two tables. Leave 1'–2' of space between cups.
- Place a plastic insect beneath each cup.
- Create an insect wand by attaching stickers or plastic insects to a wooden dowel or paint stirring stick. Glue a larger paper insect to the end of the wand.

WHAT TO DO

1. Include this activity as part of your daily good morning routine.
2. Begin by saying good morning to the children in the class.
3. As the children respond with "good morning," pick up the insect wand.
4. Tell the children that it's time to say "good morning" to the insects in your classroom as well.
5. Walk around the circle area and lightly tap each child on the shoulder signaling that it's their turn to say good morning to the insects at the table.
6. As the children are tapped on the shoulder, they may go up and walk in the designated direction around the table(s) to peek at each insect beneath each cup and say "good morning."
7. Encourage the children to identify each insect and say the insect name in their greeting: "Good morning, Mr. Cricket," "Good morning, Ms. Caterpillar," and so on.

ASSESSMENT

Consider the following:
- Can the children name the individual insects?
- Can the children describe the differences between the various insects?

Children's Books

Are You a Ladybug? by
  Judy Allen and
  Tudor Humphries
Ladybugs and Beetles
  by Sally Morgan
The Very Busy Spider by
  Eric Carle

Mary J. Murray, Mazomanie, WI

Smell Flowers Like a Bee

4+

LEARNING OBJECTIVES

The children will:

1. Develop their sense of smell.
2. Learn about how bees communicate.
3. Experience social interaction and cooperation.

Materials

small containers
samples of items
   with strong
   smells (vinegar,
   peanut butter,
   grated chocolate,
   lemon juice,
   peppermint,
   strong cheese,
   and so on)
wax paper
rubber bands

VOCABULARY

aroma   bee   pheromones   recognize   smell

PREPARATION

- Put a small amount of each item into each container. (**Safety note:** Be sure to check for allergies before selecting the materials to use.)
- Cut wax paper into circles. Prick holes into the circles, so it is easy to smell through them but not see through.
- Put a wax paper circle over each container and attach with a rubber band.

WHAT TO DO

1. Tell the children that they are going to learn all about bees.
2. Ask them how we recognize other people. They will probably answer that it is by how they look or how they sound.
3. Ask if they know how bees recognize each other.
4. Tell them that bees recognize one another by smell. Bees have special smells (called pheromones, if they ask), which is how they recognize each other.
5. Tell them that you've captured some smells for them, and you want to see if they recognize them.
6. Divide them into groups of two or three and give each group a different smell container.
7. Give them a chance to trade containers and experience all the smells.
8. Talk about the different smells within the bigger group.

TEACHER-TO-TEACHER TIP

- If a child cannot distinguish between the smells at age four, this may be a symptom of a sensory deficiency or medical condition.

Children's Books

The Bee-Man of Orn by
   Frank R. Stockton
Buzz Said the Bee by
   Wendy Cheyette
   Lewison
*The Honey Bee and the
   Robber* by Eric Carle

ASSESSMENT

Consider the following:

- Ask the children how bees recognize each other.
- Can the children recognize basic aromas?
- Can the children describe how bees cooperate with one another?

Anne Adeney, Plymouth, United Kingdom

Spiders

4+

LEARNING OBJECTIVES

The children will:
1. Learn that some spiders are dangerous and some are not.
2. Learn never to touch a spider.
3. Learn about the importance of spiders.
4. Enhance their vocabulary and language skills.

Materials

paper
crayons
color photographs
  of spiders

VOCABULARY

arachnid	leg	web
insect	spider	

PREPARATION

- Place the items from the materials list on the children's work tables.

WHAT TO DO

1. Sit in a circle and ask the children what they know or feel about spiders. Ask them to complete the sentence: "When I see a spider I _____."
2. Explain that insects have six legs and spiders have eight. Spiders are not insects; they are arachnids. We should never touch spiders. We don't want to hurt them and some might bite. Talk about the importance of spiders to the environment.
3. Read one of the books and then talk with the children about what they learned.
4. At the tables, have the children draw pictures about spiders.

POEM

Little Spider by Shirley Anne Ramaley
I see a little spider
Spin a web next to a tree.
It works so hard all day long,
But I don't think it sees me.

ASSESSMENT

Consider the following:
- Ask the children if they think spiders are important.
- Can they tell you if spiders are insects? Should they ever touch or disturb spiders?

Children's Books

Are You a Spider? by Tudor Humphries
The Eensy-Weensy Spider by Mary Ann Hoberman and Nadine Bernard Westcott
The Itsy Bitsy Spider by Iza Trapani
Little Miss Spider by David Kirk
Time for Kids: Spiders! by the Editors of Time for Kids

Shirley Anne Ramaley, Sun City, AZ

The Web of Life

4+

LEARNING OBJECTIVES

The children will:
1. Cooperate with peers in the creation of an interesting structure.
2. Develop their small motor skills.

Materials

large ball of brightly colored yarn

VOCABULARY

catch	spin	throw	web
hold	sticky	toss	yarn
pass	support		

WHAT TO DO

1. Engage the children in a conversation about spider webs. Ask the children to describe what spiders use their webs for.
2. Have the children sit in a circle and explain that they're going to be spinning a spider's web. Ask them to pretend that their hands are very sticky to hold the thread tightly, like a spider.
3. Give the ball of yarn to the first child and invite him to say something that he likes about spiders.
4. Keeping a firm grip on the loose end of yarn, have him use his other hand to toss the ball of yarn across the circle to the child sitting opposite. This child will hold the line and speak about spiders if he wishes, then throw the ball across the circle to a classmate while holding on to his end tightly.
5. Eventually a web will emerge. Finally, see if the web will support a stuffed toy resting on the top.

TEACHER-TO-TEACHER TIP

- Most young children have trouble throwing accurately, so this activity works better with smaller circles (10–15 children). Also, from time to time a child might let go of his line and need to retrieve it, so be ready to assist.

SONG

- Say the nursery rhyme "Little Miss Muffett" with the children.

ASSESSMENT

Consider the following:
- Do the children understand the concept of webs?
- Are the children able to create the web successfully?
- Are the children able to work together well?

Children's Books

Anansi Does the Impossible! An Ashanti Tale retold by Verna Aardema
Bug IQ by Roger Priddy
Roberto, the Insect Architect by Nina Laden

Patrick Mitchell, Yagoto, Nagoya, Japan

What Is Your Favorite Insect?

LEARNING OBJECTIVES

The children will:
1. Learn about insects.
2. Learn about comparison and selection.

Materials

tagboard for the header card
pictures of bugs
computer or marker
name cards for each child in the class
pocket chart

VOCABULARY

ant	choose	favorite
bee	count	grasshopper
butterfly	dragonfly	ladybug

PREPARATION

● Create a header card for the pocket chart that says, "What is your favorite insect?" Put pictures of various insects with their names printed underneath across the top of the pocket chart.

WHAT TO DO

1. At circle or group time, place the header card in the top row of a pocket chart.
2. Ask each child to pick her favorite insect and place her name card under the insect of her choice on the pocket chart.
3. Encourage the children to gather in groups based on which insect they choose. Challenge them to count how many people they have in their groups.

What is your favorite insect?			
Ant	Bee	Ladybug	Butterfly
Paul	Kia	Mylo	Zack
Amal	Ben	Ben	Liz
			Asia

TEACHER-TO-TEACHER TIP

● You can find cute insect pictures on the Internet. Instead of using name cards and a pocket chart, you can make a chart on chart paper and write the children's names under their favorite insect.

ASSESSMENT

Consider the following:
● How well do the children participate in the activity?
● Do the children listen attentively with sustained interest?

Children's Books

Look Closer by Brian and Rebecca Wildsmith
Miss Spider's Tea Party by David Kirk
The Very Hungry Caterpillar by Eric Carle

Jackie Wright, Enid, OK

Flutter-Hop Game

3+

LEARNING OBJECTIVES

The children will:
1. Develop their large motor skills.
2. Make movement transitions.
3. Develop their listening skills.

Materials

pictures of grasshoppers and butterflies or the actual bugs in ventilated jars
masking tape

VOCABULARY

butterfly	flutter	hop	jar	start
finish	grasshopper	imitate	move	

PREPARATION

- In a large, open indoor area, place the pictures or jars where the children can readily see them.
- Put a long strip of masking tape on the floor to mark the game's starting line.
- Place a strip of masking tape at the other end of the room for the finish line.

WHAT TO DO

1. Show the pictures or jars of each insect and explain that each one moves differently.
2. Select a child to imitate how to hop like a grasshopper or flutter like a butterfly.
3. Teach them the Flutter-Hop Game. Have the children at one end of the selected area with their toes on the masking tape line.
4. As you alternately call out "Grasshoppers!" or "Butterflies!" the children all hop or flutter appropriately toward the finish line.
5. Make it really fun by calling for several transitions between hopping and fluttering so the children have to pay close attention and make the appropriate movement change.
6. Turn the insects loose after the children have enjoyed watching them for a short while. Explain that the insects need to be released to get air, food, and water.

TEACHER-TO-TEACHER TIP

- Use this as a transition when moving from one area to another or from one activity to another. For example: "All those wearing green, please hop to the snack area," or "Anyone whose name begins with T, please flutter over and line up for recess."

ASSESSMENT

Consider the following:
- Do the children make appropriate movements to represent different insects?
- Do the children make proper transitions from hopping or fluttering?

Kay Flowers, Summerfield, OH

Children's Books

Butterflies by Karen Shapiro
Butterfly, Butterfly by Petr Horacek
Velma Gratch and the Way Cool Butterfly by Alan Madison

Birthday Bug Bags

4+

LEARNING OBJECTIVES

The children will:
1. Improve their social skills.
2. Learn to identify various insects.
3. Enhance their vocabularies.

Materials

2 birthday gift bags,
  10" or larger
6 stuffed or
  beanbag toy
  insects
2 sheets colored
  tissue paper
insect stickers

VOCABULARY

antenna	eye	happy birthday	insect	name
bug	gift bag	identify	leg	wing

PREPARATION

- Place three toy insects inside each bag.
- Attach several insect stickers to the outside of each bag.
- Stuff a piece of colored tissue paper on top of the toy insects, so that it "puffs" out the top of the bag (like a birthday gift).

WHAT TO DO

1. Invite pairs of children to play this "Birthday Bug Bag" game.
2. Each child selects a birthday gift bag.
3. The first player gives a birthday bag to the other child and says "Happy bug birthday!"
4. The player receives the bag, says, "Thank you!" and then removes the tissue paper and removes and identifies each insect.
5. That child then says, "Happy bug birthday!" to the other child and hands her the other gift bag. This child removes and identifies the bugs in her bag.
6. When the children finish, they mix up the insects, put three inside each bag, and top it with the tissue paper, so the game is ready for the next players.

TEACHER-TO-TEACHER TIP

- Add more than three insects to each bag or use small gift bags containing pictures, stickers, or small plastic insects in place of the stuffed/beanbag toys.

ASSESSMENT

Consider the following:
- Place an assortment of insects in each bag. Have a child remove each insect one by one, identify it, describe it, and then display the group of insects in categories according to color, type, or size.
- Display a birthday card in a box along with an assortment of bugs. Invite the child to say, "Happy bug birthday!" to each bug as she identifies each insect.

Children's Books

Bees, Bugs, and Beetles by Ronald N. Rood
The Best Book of Bugs by Claire Llewellyn
More Bugs in Boxes by David A. Carter

Mary J. Murray, Mazomanie, WI

Bugs on the Rug

4+

LEARNING OBJECTIVES

The children will:
1. Identify shapes.
2. Improve their motor skills.
3. Recognize colors.

Materials

construction paper
   in a variety of
   colors
scissors (adult use
   only)
black marker

VOCABULARY

| bug | crawl | turn over |
| color | numbers | |

PREPARATION

- Cut at least 30 4" paper ovals from the construction paper.
- Use the marker to draw a face and a number or letter on one side of each paper circle.
- Lay the paper "bugs" face down randomly about the large group area.

WHAT TO DO

1. Talk with the children about the way bugs walk. Talk about the word "crawl" and ask if they can show you what it means. Then talk about how some bugs can fly also, and ask the children to show you how bugs might fly.
2. Tell the children that when you say, "Ready, set, go buggy!" they should crawl around the floor like a bug, and turn over each paper bug they come upon.
3. Ask them to name the letter or number on the bottom side of each bug they see and then turn it back over.
4. Allow several minutes for the children to identify shapes as they crawl around.
5. Call, "Fly away home," directing the children to "fly" to their starting place.

ASSESSMENT

Consider the following:
- Invite one child to lay out a string of 10 paper "bugs." Listen and observe as the child turns over each paper bug and identifies each letter or number.
- Gather all 30 of the paper bugs together. Place them in a butterfly net. As you hold the net, have the children come forward one by one to remove a bug from the net, show the class, and then name the letter or number. Continue until all the bugs have been removed from the net and each letter or number has been identified.

Mary J. Murray, Mazomanie, WI

Children's Books

Bugs Are Best! by
   Ruth Thomas
*I Like Bugs:
the Sound of B* by Alice
   K. Flanagan
*The Very Hungry
Caterpillar* by Eric Carle

Buzzin' Bees

4+

LEARNING OBJECTIVES

The children will:
1. Identify pictures and beginning sounds.
2. Identify body parts.
3. Learn to play a new game.

Materials

pictures of ordinary
  objects and
  animals
4 pictures of a bee
tagboard
marker
glue stick
child-safe scissors

VOCABULARY

bee	buzz	elbow	nose	toe
body	ear	knee	sound	

PREPARATION

- Create a set of picture cards to use in a flash card game. On most cards, draw or glue pictures of ordinary objects and animals. On at least four of the cards, put a picture of a bee and print the word "BUZZ."

WHAT TO DO

1. Talk with the children about bees. Ask the children to describe the sound that bees make, and how it differs from the sounds other insects make.
2. Shuffle all the cards together.
3. Flip through the cards one at a time, and ask the children to identify the pictures and beginning sounds.
4. When you come to a bee card, everyone jumps up and "buzzes" around, pretending to be bees.
5. Call out the name of a part of the body, like knees. Have the children stop and touch their knees gently to another child's knees and freeze in that position.
6. When everyone is in the freeze position with knees touching, ask them to sit down.
7. Continue the game as before.

ASSESSMENT

Consider the following:
- Observe how the children are able to name the pictures correctly and give the correct beginning sounds.
- Do they listen and follow directions and display knowledge of body parts?

Jackie Wright, Enid, OK

Children's Books

Berlioz the Bear by
Jan Brett
*The Honeybee and the
Robber* by Eric Carle
Honeybees by
Jane Lecht

Capture a Bug

4+

LEARNING OBJECTIVES

The children will:
1. Identify color.
2. Learn to cooperate.
3. Improve their ability to follow directions.

Materials

images of flies and ladybugs
red and black socks or mittens of varying size (use other colors for other insects, if desired)
plastic margarine or whipped topping containers, 16 oz. or larger
basket or box

VOCABULARY

black	catch	describe	ladybug	underneath
bug	color	fly	red	
capture	cover	insect	toss	

PREPARATION

- Roll each sock or mitten inside of itself, creating a ball-shaped "bug."
- Place the sock bugs and the stack of containers inside the basket.

WHAT TO DO

1. Show the children images of flies and ladybugs. Ask the children to describe the characteristics of each.
2. Show the children the socks in the basket. Tell the children that the red socks will represent ladybugs, while the black socks will represent flies.
3. Select a "bug" from the basket.
4. Call out a child's name and invite that child to catch the bug as you toss it into the air. Challenge the child to say what kind of "bug" it is.
5. After distributing the bugs, invite the children to form a large circle and place their bugs randomly about the floor.
6. Then select a child to "capture" a bug.
7. Provide the child with a plastic container and give a direction such as, "Joseph, capture a ladybug," or "Sophie, please capture a fly."
8. Continue the bug-catching activity as the children show their ability to identify colors and follow directions, covering each bug with a container.
9. After capturing the bugs, ask the children to lift a container and identify the color of the bug hiding underneath.

ASSESSMENT

Consider the following:
- Can the children identify the colors of the socks by name?
- How well do the children work together and take turns identifying the sock bugs' colors?

Children's Books

Blue Bug's Book of Colors by Virginia Poulet
Flying Colors: Butterflies in Your Backyard by Nancy Loewen
More Bugs in Boxes by David A. Carter

Mary J. Murray, Mazomanie, WI

Catch a Fly

4+

LEARNING OBJECTIVES

The children will:
1. Learn about spider behavior.
2. Develop listening and patience skills.

Materials

blindfold (optional)

VOCABULARY

listening	sitting	waiting
pointing	spider web	

WHAT TO DO

1. Have the children sit in a circle and choose one child (the spider) to sit in the center wearing a blindfold (or with closed eyes).
2. Have another child (the fly) slowly and quietly approach the child in the center of the circle.
3. Have the approaching child (the fly) makes a buzzing sound. The child in the center of the circle (the spider) should try to identify the direction of the sound by pointing in the direction of the sound.
4. After several approaches, have the "spider" child return to the circle.
5. Choose another child to sit in the spider's web.

TEACHER-TO-TEACHER TIP

- Using the blindfold heightens the children's interest in most any activity. For those children who prefer not to wear the blindfold, this activity may be done with closed eyes.

ASSESSMENT

Consider the following:
- Are the children sitting in the circle engaged during the activity? Do they enjoy hushing one another as "the fly" approaches?
- Do the children interact well together?

Children's Books

Flying Insects by Patricia Lantier-Sampon
Old Black Fly by Jim Aylesworth
There Was an Old lady Who Swallowed a Fly by Pam Adams

Patrick Mitchell, Yagoto, Nagoya, Japan

Meet My Flying Friend

4+

LEARNING OBJECTIVES

The children will:
1. Identify bugs.
2. Learn a poem about bugs.
3. Play a game involving bugs.

Materials

pictures of winged
    insects
cardstock
glue stick
marker

VOCABULARY

bee	firefly	ladybug	moth
dragonfly	fly	mosquito	rhyme

PREPARATION

● Make a set of insect cards. Fold pieces of cardstock in the middle so that they will stand up. Glue the image of an insect on one side, and write the insect's name on the other side of the cardstock.

WHAT TO DO

1. Place the insect cards on the floor in a circle.
2. Teach the children the following rhyme, and have the children skip around the insect cards as you recite it together. Name a different insect in each blank:

   Meet My Friend by anonymous
   Meet my friend, little Mr. _____.
   He's a buzzy, busy little guy.
   Meet my friend, little Mr. _____.
   He can crawl and he can fly.
   Meet my friend, little Mr. _____.
   See how he zips through the air.
   Meet my friend, little Mr. _____.
   With his wings, he can travel anywhere.

3. When the rhyme mentions an insect, the child beside the correct insect card picks it up and shows it to the rest of the children.
4. Repeat the activity a few times, changing the order in which you name the insects.

ASSESSMENT

Consider the following:
● How well do the children participate in the game?
● Do the children correctly identify each insect?

Jackie Wright, Enid, OK

Children's Books

Miss Spider's Tea Party by David Kirk
Old Black Fly by Jim Aylesworth
The Very Lonely Firefly by Eric Carle

Crickets and Grasshoppers 4+

LEARNING OBJECTIVES

The children will:
1. Lean to make observations.
2. Improve their large motor skills.
3. Practice taking turns.

Materials

picture of a cricket
picture of a
  grasshopper
books about
  crickets and
  grasshoppers
live cricket or
  grasshopper

VOCABULARY

chirp	fly	jump	same
cricket	grasshopper	notice	sound
different	hop	observe	

WHAT TO DO

1. Gather the children and show them the pictures of the cricket and grasshopper.
2. Invite the children to comment on the appearance of each insect and encourage them to share what they already know about crickets or grasshoppers.
3. Invite one or more children to demonstrate how a cricket might sound and how it might hop about. Invite another child to demonstrate how a grasshopper might jump about the classroom.
4. Divide the class into two groups. Assign one group to be the crickets and the other group to be the grasshoppers.
5. Have all the children line up at the far side of the room with one or two feet of space between each child.
6. Take turns displaying a cricket or grasshopper picture and saying commands such as, "Crickets hop three times," or "Grasshoppers jump twice."
7. Continue calling out commands until all the crickets and grasshoppers are sitting at your feet.
8. Share one of the books with the children and then repeat the activity.

TEACHER-TO-TEACHER TIP

- Make copies of the cricket and grasshopper pictures. Give each child a picture to hold as they hop or jump across the room.

ASSESSMENT

Consider the following:
- Invite a child to page through one of the books suggested in the list on this page. Listen as the child "teaches" you what she knows about crickets or grasshoppers.
- Can the children describe the similarities and differences between crickets and grasshoppers?

Children's Books

Crickets and Grasshoppers by Ann O. Squire
Discovering Crickets and Grasshoppers by Keith Porter
The Very Quiet Cricket by Eric Carle

Mary J. Murray, Mazomanie, WI

Fireflies

4+

LEARNING OBJECTIVES

The children will:

1. Demonstrate what "over," "under," and "beside" mean by using a flashlight.
2. Understand that fireflies get their names because they are luminescent.

flashlights (1 per child, or enough for pairs of children to share)

VOCABULARY

beside	flashlight	over
firefly	luminescent	under

PREPARATION

- Read books about fireflies (see list for suggestions).

WHAT TO DO

1. Have the children sit together on the floor.
2. Engage the children in a discussion about fireflies. Ask the children if they have seen fireflies before, and if so, why the insects have such an interesting name.
3. Hand out several flashlights. Tell the children their flashlights are fireflies and you are going to make the room dark.
4. Take turns. Have a child place their firefly over, under, and beside an object.

POEM

Holding the Light by Kristen Peters

I cup my hands, fingers wrapped tight,   *Shall I set my fireflies free?*
A crawling insect gives me fright!   *A pleasing show of lights I see!*

TEACHER-TO-TEACHER TIPS

- Take a Popsicle™ stick and paint it with glow-in-the-dark paint. Make wings with wax paper. Draw on eyes. Turn off the lights and have the fireflies dance to classical music.
- Play "freeze dance" with glow sticks (with the lights off) to the song "Firefly" by Nancy Stewart or any other music. When you turn the lights on, have the children freeze.

ASSESSMENT

Consider the following:

- Do the children understand why fireflies have the name they do?
- Can the children shine their flashlights over, under, and beside an object when directed?

Children's Books

Fireflies by Julie Brinckloe
Fireflies, Fireflies Light My Way by Jonathan London
The Very Lonely Firefly by Eric Carle

Kristen Peters, Mattituck, NY

Fly Like a Butterfly

4+

LEARNING OBJECTIVES

The children will:
1. Identify creatures in pictures.
2. Name beginning sounds.
3. Learn to play a new game.

Materials

4 pictures of a
    butterfly
marker
cardstock cut into
    flash card size
glue stick
child-safe scissors

VOCABULARY

butterfly	directions	flutter	move
card	flip	fly	

PREPARATION

● Create a set of cards to use in a flash card game. On at least four of the cards print a picture of a butterfly with the words "Fly like a butterfly." On the other cards, print the letters of the alphabet.

WHAT TO DO

1. Shuffle all the cards together.
2. Flip through the cards one at a time, asking the children to identify the letters.
3. When you come to a butterfly card, everyone stands up and flies around like a butterfly. Talk with the children about how butterflies move.

TEACHER-TO-TEACHER TIP

● Instead of butterflies, use different animal pictures and movements: slithering snakes, hopping bunnies, swimming fish, and so on. Instead of letters of the alphabet, use sight words or pictures.

ASSESSMENT

Consider the following:
● Are the children able to identify the letters they see on the cards?
● Do the children move like butterflies when they see the appropriate card?

Jackie Wright, Enid, OK

Children's Books

A Butterfly Is Born by
    Melvin Berger
*I Wish I Were
a Butterfly* by
James Howe
*A Monarch
Butterfly's Life* by
John Himmelman
*The Very Hungry
Caterpillar* by Eric Carle

Insect Cards

4+

LEARNING OBJECTIVES

The children will:
1. Identify insects.
2. Follow directions.

images of insects
laminator

VOCABULARY

ant	cicada	fly	moth	termite
bee	cockroach	grasshopper	praying	wasp
butterfly	dragonfly	ladybug	mantis	
caterpillar	firefly	mosquito	stag beetle	

PREPARATION

- Locate some attractive and brightly colored insect pictures that are about 3" × 4".
- Laminate and cut off any sharp corners.

WHAT TO DO

1. Show the cards one at a time and ask the children to say the names of the insects. Help the children if necessary.
2. Have the children repeat the names of the insects as you show the cards.
3. Spread the cards out face up on the floor or table.
4. Call out the name of an insect and the name of a child. This child runs to pick up that card.
5. Continue with the remaining cards and children.

MORE TO DO

- For a language exercise, display the cards and ask a child, "What insect do you like?" The child chooses an insect card and says, "I like beetles. How about you?" The children can learn to manage this simple dialogue/activity themselves.

TEACHER-TO-TEACHER TIP

- These versatile cards can also be backed with self-adhesive magnetic strips so that they stick on a magnetic surface.

ASSESSMENT

Consider the following:
- Can the children identify certain insects, when prompted?
- Do the children pick up the correct insect cards?

Patrick Mitchell, Yagoto, Nagoya, Japan

Children's Books

Bugs! Bugs! Bugs! by Bob Barner
Flying Insects by Patricia Lantier-Sampon
My Bug Book by Melissa Stewart

Insect Dominoes

4+

LEARNING OBJECTIVES

The children will:
1. Choose an activity without the help of a teacher.
2. Demonstrate ability to take turns and play cooperatively.
3. Focus on an activity for a reasonable length of time to complete the game.
4. Identify and match insect pictures.

Materials

tagboard
marker
insect pictures or
    stickers
child-safe scissors

VOCABULARY

ant	caterpillar	fly	praying mantis
beetle	cricket	lightning bug	wasp
butterfly	dragonfly	moth	

WHAT TO DO

1. Prepare the desired number of tagboard rectangles with center lines to resemble dominoes.
2. Apply self-adhesive insect stickers or glue insect pictures on each end of the dominoes.
3. Have the children use these dominoes to play the traditional game of dominoes or create their own games by matching identical insects on the dominoes.

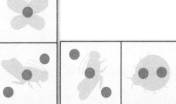

TEACHER-TO-TEACHER TIP

● Laminate the dominoes for durability.

ASSESSMENT

Consider the following:
● Do the children show an increase in their ability to use one-to-one correspondence in matching identical insects?
● Do children display increased control of the small muscles in their hands, and improved eye-hand coordination?
● Do the children show improvement in their ability to play cooperatively with other children?

Jackie Wright, Enid, OK

Children's Books

The Best Book of Bugs by Claire Llewellyn
The Bug Book by William Dugan
Miss Spider's Tea Party by David Kirk

Match the Insects

4+

LEARNING OBJECTIVES

The children will:
1. Develop their matching skills.
2. Increase their memory.
3. Become familiar with the concepts "same" and "different."

Materials

insect stickers (two
   sets)
juice can lids
   (enough to make
   two of each
   insect)
magnetic wands

VOCABULARY

bug	insect	match	names of	pair	wand
different	lid	memory	insects	same	

PREPARATION

- Ahead of time, put one insect sticker on each juice lid, making sure each lid has a match (you are making an insect memory game).

WHAT TO DO

1. Give each child a lid and then have him find the child who has the match to his insect. Ask the children to give other children clues about their insects before looking to see if their lids match. For example, "My insect is red and black," or "My insect has colorful wings."
2. Place all of the lids out on the floor face up and ask the children to find pairs.
3. For older children, play a "memory" game: Place the lids face down on the floor and tell the children to turn the lids over one at a time and try to remember which insect lid is which. If they turn two over that don't match, they turn them both face down again. If the lids match, the children can pick them up.

TEACHER-TO-TEACHER TIP

- Play the game with them for the first few times and then let them try on their own. You might also send the game home with them so that they can play with their families.

SONGS

Sing "The Ants Go Marching" or "Ten Little Butterflies" with the children.

ASSESSMENT

Consider the following:
- Can the children go from matching with the lids facing up to turning them over where they can't see the stickers?
- Can the children name some of the insects if shown images? Can the children describe an insect if you say the insect's name?

Holly Dzierzanowski, Brenham, TX

Children's Books

The Best Book of Bugs
  by Claire Llewellyn
I Like Bugs by Margaret
  Wise Brown
On Beyond Bugs:
All About Insects by
  Tish Rabe
The Very Clumsy Click
Beetle by Eric Carle

Mother, May I Move Like an Insect?

4+

LEARNING OBJECTIVES

The children will:

1. Ask for permission before doing an activity.
2. Demonstrate knowledge of how various insects move.
3. Demonstrate ability to follow instructions.

Materials

VOCABULARY

bee	crawl	insect	match	travel
bug	fly	jump	move	

WHAT TO DO

1. Stand at one end of the play area. Have the children line up at the other end.
2. Explain that you are "Mother." The children must move like a particular insect or bug to your end of the play area. This could mean jumping like a grasshopper or flying like a bee.
3. Explain that they must ask your permission to travel to your end of the play area. They must ask to move like a particular insect or bug, such as "Mother, may I fly like a butterfly?"
4. Have one child begin. If the child matches a bug with the correct type of movement, say "Yes, you may." If not, say "No, you may not, but you may (correct type of movement)." For example, if the child asks "Mother, may I jump like a bee," you would say "No, you may not, but you may fly like a bee."
5. The child will then fly, jump, or run to your end of the play area.
6. Repeat until all the children have had a turn.

TEACHER-TO-TEACHER TIP

* Challenge the children to imagine how a certain insect might move, and then have the children act out those movements.

Children's Books

The Best Book of Bugs by Claire Llewellyn
Bugs, Bugs, Bugs by Bob Barner
I Like Bugs by Margaret Wise Brown

ASSESSMENT

Consider the following:

* Are the children able to ask for permission?
* Are the children able to match an insect with a movement?
* Are the children able to follow your directions?

Sue Bradford Edwards, Florissant, MO

Smell Out Your Group!

LEARNING OBJECTIVES

The children will:
1. Develop their sense of smell.
2. Learn how bees communicate.
3. Experience social interaction and cooperation.

Materials

small containers
 (1 for each child)
samples of strong-
 smelling foods,
 such as vinegar,
 peanut butter,
 and and so on
wax paper
scissors
rubber bands

VOCABULARY

aroma   recognize   smell

PREPARATION

- Put small amounts of each food into containers. (**Safety note:** Check for children's allergies before picking the foods for this activity.) The number of different foods you use depends on the number of children you have. Four will do for 8–12 children, six for 12–18, while eight extends to 16–24 children.
- Cut circles out of wax paper. Prick holes into the wax paper, so the contents are easy to smell.
- Fasten a circle over the top of each substance container with a rubber band. **Safety Note:** Be sure none of the children have a peanut allergy before introducing peanut butter to the classroom.

WHAT TO DO

1. Tell the children that bees use smells to recognize each other.
2. First give the children opportunities to practice smelling the containers.
3. Then, have the children spread out around the room, giving each child a smelling container.
4. Ask the children to sniff the container and then "smell out" the other child or children with the same smell. Their smelly containers and their noses will help them find and join the vinegar group, or the peanut butter group.
5. Tell them to find their partners just by smelling each other's aroma containers.

TEACHER-TO-TEACHER TIP

- Use this game as a fun transition to get the children into partners or groups before an activity.

ASSESSMENT

Consider the following:
- Can the children identify by smell only?
- Are the children able to use the smells to find their partners?
- Do the children cooperate with each other in the activity?

Children's Books

The Bee Tree by Patricia Polacco
Beekeepers by Linda Oatman High
Belinda Bee's Busy Year by Rusty Wise

Anne Adeney, Plymouth, United Kingdom

Where's That Bug?

4+

LEARNING OBJECTIVES

The children will:

1. Become familiar with positional vocabulary terms.
2. Develop their visual memory skills.

Materials

sheet of poster
   board
masking tape
cutouts of various
   insects and bugs

VOCABULARY

below   beside   near   over   pond   under

PREPARATION

- Color or cover the poster board to look like an outdoor pond scene by making a sky, a pond, trees, grass, flowers, and so on.
- Cut out or print pictures of different insects in sizes that will fit on your board (make sure they are large enough for the children to hold, but not too large for your poster).
- Put a masking tape loop on the back of each insect and attach the insects to various areas of your poster. Place some in the sky, on a tree, beside a flower, or above the pond.

WHAT TO DO

1. Set up the poster in your classroom. Explain the scene to your class. Tell the children to study the picture to remember where the insects are.
2. After a couple of minutes, remove the insects and place them on the floor.
3. Ask each child to pick up an insect, try to remember where it was, and put it back in that spot.
4. For a language component, give each child an insect and tell him where to put it by using positional words such as "put it *beside* a tree, put it *in* the sky, and put it *over* the pond."

SONG

- Sing "The Ants Go Marching" with the children.

TEACHER-TO-TEACHER TIP

- Try starting with fewer insects, and then add more.

ASSESSMENT

Consider the following:

- Can the children use positional vocabulary to describe an insect's location?
- Can the children recall and describe the location of various insects at a later time?

Children's Books

Belinda Bee's Busy Year by Rusty Wise
Come See My Bugs by Rozanne Williams
The Honeybee and the Robber by Eric Carle

Suzanne Maxymuk, Cherry Hill, NJ

Ladybug Counting Game

5+

LEARNING OBJECTIVES

The children will:
1. Begin to identify numbers.
2. Begin to learn how to count.

Materials

construction paper
  (red and black)
glue stick
child-safe scissors
index cards
markers

VOCABULARY

count	match	number names
ladybug	number	spot

PREPARATION

- Cut out 10 ladybugs from red construction paper and cut spots out of black construction paper.
- Write the numbers from 1–10 on the index cards. Glue spots on the ladybugs, so you have a set from 1–10 to match the cards.

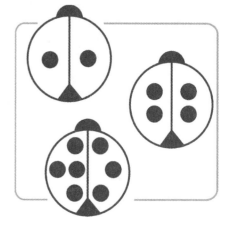

WHAT TO DO

1. Gather the children together in a group. Engage them in a conversation about ladybugs. Ask the children to describe how ladybugs look.
2. Show the children the ladybugs on the wall in the classroom. With the children, count the number of dots on each ladybug's back.
3. Set out the numbered index cards.
4. Ask each child to come forward and select a card.
5. Challenge each child to identify the number on the card she picks. Make sure that all of the children can see the number as well.
6. Ask the child who picked the card to match it to the ladybug with the same number of spots on its back.
7. Repeat with all the children.

ASSESSMENT

Consider the following:
- Can the children identify the numbers on their cards?
- Can the children match the numbers on their cards to the correct ladybugs?

Children's Books

Chicka, Chicka, One, Two, Three by Bill Martin, Jr. and Michael Sampson
The Grouchy Ladybug by Eric Carle
Ten Little Ladybugs by Melanie Girth and Laura Huliska-Beith

Hilary Romig, Las Cruces, NM

Insect Name Matchup

4+

LEARNING OBJECTIVES

The children will:

1. Learn to identify insects by sight.
2. Identify the letters in insects' names, and try to read the names of insects.

Materials

- index cards
- marker
- pictures of various insects
- glue stick
- chalk
- chalkboard
- eraser

VOCABULARY

ant	cricket	grasshopper	moth
bee	dragonfly	matching	wasp

PREPARATION

- On each of the cards, write the name of an insect, and glue a picture of that insect to the other side of the word card.

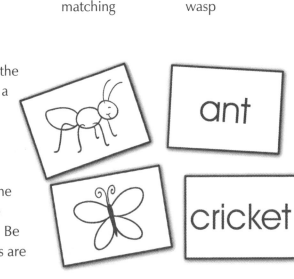

WHAT TO DO

1. Display the insect cards on the chalkrail or on the rug so the children can see them easily. Be sure the images of the insects are facing up.
2. Choose one insect name and write it on the lower half of the chalkboard. Sound out the name with the children.
3. Ask a child to find the card with the image of that insect on it.
4. Flip the insect card over and hold it next to the written word on the chalkboard and ask the children to make sure it is a match.
5. Ask the children to say the name of each letter in the insect's name. Challenge them further to try to spell the insect's name.
6. Repeat, leaving the words written on the board.
7. To erase the words at the end of the activity, ask a child to choose a name card and find and erase the matching word on the board.

Children's Books

Fireflies in the Night by Judy Hawes
The Very Hungry Caterpillar by Eric Carle
The Very Quiet Cricket by Eric Carle
What About Ladybugs? by Celia Godkin

ASSESSMENT

Consider the following:

- Can the children identify images of insects by name?
- Can the children identify the letters in each insect's name?
- Can the children read an insect's name with help?

Susan Oldham Hill, Lakeland, FL

Jars

4+

LEARNING OBJECTIVES

The children will:
1. Develop their small motor skills.
2. Identify various insects.
3. Identify colors.
4. Improve their vocabulary skills.

Materials

6 or more wide-mouth, clean, clear plastic jars with lids (peanut butter or mayonnaise jars work well for this activity)

6 or more beanbag insects

basket

VOCABULARY

bug	insect	lid	spill
close	jar	open	tight

PREPARATION

- Stuff one beanbag insect inside each jar.
- Attach each lid and screw it on tightly.
- Display the jars in a basket in the classroom.

WHAT TO DO

1. Ask one child to select a jar.
2. Have the child unscrew the lid and remove the insect.
3. Invite the child to name the insect and describe its color, size, shape, and so on.
4. Have the child select another jar and repeat the activity until all the jars have been opened and each insect is displayed near its own jar.
5. Tell the child to place each insect back in its jar and attach the lid tightly so the activity is ready for the next child.

SONG

What's Inside this Jar? by Mary J. Murray
(Tune: "1, 2, 3, 4, 5, I Caught a Fish Alive")

What's inside this jar?   *Oh, what kind of insect*
I wonder what I'll see?   *Is waiting there for me?*

ASSESSMENT

Consider the following:

- Display the six jars in front of the class. Invite six children to come forward and ask each to choose a jar to open. Observe the child's small motor skills as he opens the jar and removes the insect. Listen as each child tells about the insect in his jar.
- Fill a shoebox with an assortment of beanbag insects or paper insects. Invite a child to remove each insect one at a time. Encourage the child to tell about the type of insect, where it might live, what it eats, and so on.

Mary J. Murray, Mazomanie, WI

Children's Books

The Best Bug Parade by Stuart Murphy
Big Bugs by Mary Gribbin
Bugs! by David Greenberg

Literacy and Bees

4+

LEARNING OBJECTIVES

The children will:
1. Learn about bees.
2. Learn to match lowercase with uppercase letters.

Materials

bee pattern
beehive pattern
scissors (adult use
   only)
yellow and tan
   paper
yarn

VOCABULARY

bee   hive   uppercase
directions   lowercase

PREPARATION

- Read books about bees with the children.
- Trace bee outlines on yellow paper, write a lowercase letter on each and cut them out. **Note:** Make several more bee outlines than beehive outlines.
- Trace beehive outlines on tan paper, write an uppercase letter on each and cut them out.
- Cut yarn and attach it to the cutouts so that the children can wear them as costumes.

WHAT TO DO

1. Gather the children together and engage them in a discussion about bees.
2. Explain that bees live together in hives, and that most bees spend their days collecting flower pollen to bring to the hive to help make honey. Also explain that bees will give one another directions to the best flowers by dancing and other body movements.
3. Set out the bee and beehive patterns, and select different children to wear them. Explain that each bee's hive is the one with the matching uppercase letter on it.
4. Have the children mix around together. After a few moments, tell the bees to fly home. Encourage the children to help one another by using gestures to direct one another how to get back to the correct hives.

ASSESSMENT

Consider the following:
- Can the children describe where bees live, and what they are doing flying around all day?
- Can the children match lowercase letters to the correct uppercase letters?

Kristen Peters, Mattituck, NY

Children's Books

The Beautiful Bee Book
   by Sue Unstead
Bumblebee by
Margaret Wise Brown
The Bumblebee Book
by Julia Mechan-Rogers
*Ruby Lee the
   Bumblebee* by
Dawn Matheson

Rhyming Caterpillars

4+

LEARNING OBJECTIVES

The children will:
1. Develop their rhyming skills.
2. Identify the names of the objects and things they see in pictures.

Materials

small paper plates
pictures of things
whose names
rhyme: cat, bat,
mat, hat; nose,
rose, hose, toes
Note: Each group
of rhyming words
should contain at
least four
pictures.
glue

VOCABULARY

bat	hose	rose
cat	mat	toes
hat	nose	

PREPARATION

● Make a caterpillar head/face on one small paper plate for each rhyming caterpillar. Glue each picture on to a paper plate.

WHAT TO DO

1. Talk with the children about how caterpillars grow. Explain that you are going to make rhyming caterpillars that will grow by finding rhyming words.
2. Begin the first caterpillar by laying out one caterpillar head.
3. Ask a child to pick out one of the plates with a picture on it and place it next to the head to start the caterpillar growing.
4. Have the next child choose a plate with a picture of a rhyming word and place it down to continue to grow the caterpillar.
5. Continue until all the pictures in that group are used.
6. Say the rhyming words together as a group.
7. Begin the next caterpillar in the same way, using a new group of rhyming words.
8. Again, build a caterpillar by adding only the plates with pictures of rhyming words.

ASSESSMENT

Consider the following:
● Do the children understand the basic concept of rhyme?
● Can the children match rhyming words together?

Suzanne Maxymuk, Cherry Hill, NJ

Children's Books

Angelina and the Butterfly by Katharine Holabird
Ten Loopy Caterpillars by Joy Cowley
The Very Hungry Caterpillar by Eric Carle

Two Halves Make a Whole Bug

LEARNING OBJECTIVES

The children will:

1. Develop visual discrimination skills.
2. Learn various insects' names.

Materials

photos of insects
scissors (adult use
   only)
laminator (optional)
box

VOCABULARY

half   halves   match   whole

PREPARATION

● Choose some colorful and attractive insect pictures.
● On the back of each picture write the name of the insect in large, clear letters.
● Laminate and cut the picture in two. Five bugs and a total of 10 pieces to match will be enough for younger children.
● Cut off any sharp corners and put your insect card halves in a box labeled "Two Halves Make a Whole."

WHAT TO DO

1. Show the children the box and take out one card.
2. Discuss what they think this bug might be, and ask them what is unusual about the picture.
3. Teach the word "half." Select a mismatched insect card and put the two halves together. Ask, "What is strange about this combined picture?"
4. Tell the children that this second insect half does not match the first.
5. Now choose the correct matching half and ask if the insect looks right. Teach that this is a whole insect.
6. Finally, show the writing on the back of the card with the two halves of the word making a whole insect name.

TEACHER-TO-TEACHER TIP

● You can increase the difficulty by making 15 insects, giving 30 halves to match. Jagged or puzzle-like cuts would also make for greater complexity.

Children's Books

The Best Bug Parade by
   Stuart Murphy
Bugs! by
   David Greenberg
Gotta Go! Gotta Go! by
   Sam Swope

ASSESSMENT

Consider the following:

● Do the children do this matching activity alone or in small groups?
● Do the children choose to work with either language or pictures to develop their independence?

Patrick Mitchell, Yagoto, Nagoya, Japan

What Letter Sound Does Your Cricket Make?

4+

LEARNING OBJECTIVES

The children will:
1. Match letters to objects whose names start with those letters.
2. Develop their small motor skills.

Materials

pictures of crickets
clothespins
green paint
pipe cleaners
wax paper
permanent marker
green plastic grass
big box
small objects

VOCABULARY

alphabet	cricket	letter	similar
antenna	different	match	sound

PREPARATION

- Create cricket clothespins: Paint 26 or more clothespins green, add pipe-cleaner antennae and legs. Use wax paper for wings.
- Draw eyes and a letter of the alphabet on each cricket's body.
- Place plastic grass in a big box with several objects starting with different letters.

WHAT TO DO

1. Engage the children in a discussion about crickets. Show the children pictures of crickets and ask the children to describe them. Talk with the children about the sounds that crickets make.
2. Give each child a cricket clothespin.
3. Challenge the children to find an object that starts with the letter sound on the cricket's back.
4. Once the child finds such an object, the child clips his cricket onto it.

SONG

I'm a Little Cricket by Kristen Peters
(Tune: "I'm a Little Teapot")

I'm a little cricket,   *I only play music*
I hop on the ground,   *When it's night,*
I love to make music,   *So please keep it dark*
Listen for my sound.   *Don't turn on the light!*

Children's Books

As Quick as a Cricket
by Audrey Wood
Oscar and the Cricket
by Geoff Waring
The Very Quiet Cricket
by Eric Carle

ASSESSMENT

Consider the following:
- Can the children identify the letters on the "crickets" you give them?
- Can the children find objects in the room that match the sound of the letters on their "crickets?"

Kristen Peters, Mattituck, NY

Bugs in Boxes

5+

LEARNING OBJECTIVES

The children will:
1. Improve their oral language skills.
2. Develop listening skills.
3. Improve their social skills.

Materials

scissors (adult use
   only)
nature magazines
   such as *Big
   Backyard*
glue stick
6 or more boxes
   with lids, such as
   shoeboxes or
   checkbook boxes

VOCABULARY

| antennae | colors | fly | legs |
| bug | crawl | insect | wings |

PREPARATION

- Cut out large pictures of insects from nature magazines.
- Glue one large insect picture inside each box.
- Print the name of the insect on the inside of the box lid.
- Place the lid on the box.

WHAT TO DO

1. Invite two children to sit together. Ask each child to select a bug box.
2. Invite the children to open their boxes and then take turns describing the insect inside.
3. Encourage the children to identify the colors, body parts, shape, size, movement, behaviors of the insect.
4. Have the children read the name of the insect inside the box lid. Help the children read the names if necessary.
5. Have the children close their box and then give it to the partner to peek inside and read the insect name.
6. Invite the pair of children to select two different bug boxes and repeat the activity.

TEACHER-TO-TEACHER TIPS

- For added appeal, cover each box lid with colored contact paper or construction paper. Write BUG BOX on each lid.
- Prepare a large number of bug boxes. Stack the boxes in the block corner and let the children build with the boxes as they talk about the various insects.

ASSESSMENT

Consider the following:
- Can the children identify the characteristics of various insects?
- Are the children able to read the insects' names without help?

Children's Books

Billions of Bugs by
   Haris Petie
Bugs by Pat McKissack
   and Frederick
   McKissack
More Bugs in Boxes by
   David A. Carter
Pattern Bugs by
   Trudy Harris

Mary J. Murray, Mazomanie, WI

If I Were a Bug...

5+

LEARNING OBJECTIVES

The children will:
1. Talk about bugs and name their favorites.
2. Complete a sentence frame about a bug.

Materials

pictures of bugs (or let the children draw their own)
paper
glue
markers
crayons
pencils
paper fasteners or stapler

VOCABULARY

bee	caterpillar	slug	wasp
beetle	dragonfly	snail	
butterfly	fly	spider	

WHAT TO DO

1. Create a class book about bugs. Use the sentence frame "If I were a bug, I would be a _____ because_____." Let each child in class contribute a page.
2. Pass out several pages with the above text written on them, and help the children fill in the blanks. The children can write or draw anything in the second space about the insect images they paste in the first space. Ask them to write their names on their page.
3. When the children complete their pages for the book, gather all the pages and bind them together using paper fasteners or a stapler.
4. Read the class book aloud with the children at circle time.
5. Encourage the children to read the book in the library area.

ASSESSMENT

Consider the following:
- How well do the children participate in making the class book?
- Do the children listen attentively as the book is read aloud?

Jackie Wright, Enid, OK

Children's Books

The Bug Book by William Dugan
Miss Spider's Tea Party by David Kirk
More Bugs in Boxes by David A. Carter
Pattern Bugs by Trudy Harris

Ladybug Letters

5+

LEARNING OBJECTIVES

The children will:
1. Develop their literacy skills.
2. Develop their sequencing skills.

Materials

ladybug pattern
red and black
   paper
scissors (adult use
   only)
black sticker dots
white paint pen or
   correction fluid
   pen
paper fasteners
index cards
string

VOCABULARY

alphabet	ladybug	sequence
between	order	

PREPARATION

- Trace the outline of a ladybug on red construction paper. Cut halfway down the center to make two wings.
- Write a letter on the ladybug.
- Trace the ladybug onto black paper. Cut out the black underside and attach it to the wings with a paper fastener (this makes wings moveable).
- Make several of these ladybugs.
- Write several letters on smaller black circle stickers with a white pen.

WHAT TO DO

1. Read the children a book on ladybugs (see list below).
2. Talk with the children about ladybugs, asking the children to describe ladybugs.
3. Give some children the ladybug cutouts, and other children the black stickers.
4. Challenge the children with the stickers to find the ladybugs with the matching letters and put the stickers on the ladybugs to make their spots.

POEM

Ladybug by Kristen Peters
A ladybug flies in the breeze.
It lands on flowers and the trees.
Upon a leaf to take a nap,
Her gentle wings no longer flap.
Her body red with spots of black;
I love to count them on her back.

Children's Books

Are You a Ladybug? by
   Judy Allen and
   Tudor Humphries
The Grouchy Ladybug
   by Eric Carle
A Ladybug's Life by
   John Himmelman
Ten Little Ladybugs by
   Melanie Gerth and
   Laura Huliska-Beith

ASSESSMENT

Consider the following:
- Can the children identify the letters on the ladybugs?
- Can the children put the ladybug letters in the correct sequence?

Kristen Peters, Mattituck, NY

Tracing Spider-Web Letters

5+

LEARNING OBJECTIVES

The children will:
1. Practice tracing letters.
2. Explore spiders and their webs.

Materials

paper plates
hole punch (adult
    use only)
black yarn
stapler
glitter
glue
plastic spider rings

VOCABULARY

letter	spider	uppercase
lowercase	trace	web

PREPARATION
- Use a hole punch to punch holes around the edges of the paper plates.

WHAT TO DO
1. Read the children books about spiders (see list below for suggestions).
2. Engage the children in a discussion about spiders. Talk with the children about spider webs, specifically explaining that spiders weave webs to serve as shelter and a way to get food.
3. Tell the children they will be making spider-web letters. **Note:** Consider making one ahead of time so they have an example from which to work.
4. Give each child a paper plate. Help the children thread yarn through the holes around the edges and across the plate, making a spider web.
5. Provide glitter and glue and help the children make different individual letters at the centers of their spider-web plates.
6. Invite the children to put their spider rings on their fingers and trace the letters on their webs.
7. Have the children trade webs with another child and practice tracing the letters the other children put in their webs.

Children's Books

The Itsy Bitsy Spider by
    Iza Trapani
Spiders by
    Gail Gibbons
The Very Busy Spider by
    Eric Carle

ASSESSMENT
Consider the following:
- Can the children describe what spiders use their webs for?
- How well can the children trace the letters?

Kristen Peters, Mattituck, NY

Ants in Your Pants!

3+

LEARNING OBJECTIVES

The children will:

1. Use body movements to respond to verbal clues.
2. Learn the meaning of the phrase "ants in your pants."

Materials

VOCABULARY

ant	hint	pants
clue	movement	

WHAT TO DO

1. Talk with the children about how large groups of ants work and live in their anthills. Talk about how they travel in groups.
2. Ask the children to imagine what it would feel like if a group of ants walked into their pants. Tell them, "If this ever happened to me, this is what I would do…" With arms up, wiggle your wrists and fingers next to your head, bend your knees slightly, hop from one foot to the other in a circular direction, and shout, "Aaaaaaah!"
3. Explain that you'll all be doing an activity that will move and stretch your bodies. Ask the children to follow your commands. When you say, "Ants in your pants!" the children should repeat your silly dance.
4. You can say, "Touch your toes. Rub your belly. Reach for the sky. Ants in your pants!" Continue with other combinations of movements, such as "Put your hands on your head. Bend your knees. Ants in your pants!"

TEACHER-TO-TEACHER TIP

- Just for fun, repeat this activity at various times during the day.

SONG

Sing "The Ants Go Marching" with the children.

Children's Books

Ants in Your Pants: A Lift-the-Flap Counting Book by Sue Heap
Are There Ants in Your Pants? by Amy Meyer Allen
"I Can't" Said the Ant by Polly Cameron

ASSESSMENT

Consider the following:

- Do the children follow the action steps as you say them?
- Do the children stop moving like they have ants in their pants when you begin a new list of movements?

Susan Sharkey, Fletcher Hills, CA

Bugs on the Balance Beam
4+

LEARNING OBJECTIVES

The children will:
1. Develop their sense of balance.
2. Improve their social skills.
3. Learn to identify insects.

Materials

balance beam or masking tape
collection of beanbag "bugs" (or plastic or paper bug cutouts)

VOCABULARY

balance   carry   count   insect   walk

PREPARATION

- Display the collection of bugs near one end of the balance beam.
- If you don't have a balance beam, create one by adhering two six-foot strips of masking tape side by side down the length of the floor.

WHAT TO DO

1. Instruct a child to select one bug, describe it and say its name, and then balance it on the balance beam. Instruct a second child to do the same.
2. Have the children continue to take turns until all the insects are displayed along the balance beam.
3. Have the children remove the insects then choose their favorite.
4. Invite the children to take turns walking down the length of the balance beam as they carry their favorite bugs along.

SONG

- Have the children carry a beanbag bug as they walk across the balance beam singing the following song. When they reach the opposite end of the balance beam they can make their bug fly, crawl, jump, or run away.

I'm Walking with My Bug by Mary J. Murray
(Tune: "Baby bumblebee")
I'm walking with my bug on the balance beam.
Come along I'll show you what I mean.
I'm walking with my bug on the balance beam.
Whee! the bug flies [hops, crawls, runs] away.

ASSESSMENT

Consider the following:
- How well are the children able to balance on the beam?
- Are the children able to wait and take turns?

Mary J. Murray, Mazomanie, WI

Children's Books

The Bug Book by William Dugan
More Bugs in Boxes by David A. Carter
Pattern Bugs by Trudy Harris

Flying Insects

4+

LEARNING OBJECTIVES

The children will:
1. Improve their large motor skills.
2. Improve their ability to follow directions.

assorted socks

felt

scissors (adult use only)

needle and thread (adult use only)

rubber bands or yarn

cotton stuffing or extra socks

VOCABULARY

far   fly   insect   throw   wing

PREPARATION

● Create the following insect socks:
  ● *Round bug:* Make a sock ball by rolling a sock inside of itself. Cut out and stitch two felt wings to each sock ball.
  ● *Segmented worm:* Stuff a longer sock with another sock. Stitch the end closed. Knot several strands of yarn along the body, making many sections.
  ● *Three-part insect:* Stuff a sock and stitch it closed. Put two rubber bands around the body, separating it into three parts.
  ● *Funny bugs:* Stuff colorful gloves or toe socks with stuffing or a sock and stitch them closed.

WHAT TO DO

1. Gather the children outside or in a large open space.
2. Talk with the children about different kinds of insects. Ask the children how various insects move and get around.
3. Show the children the various insect sock creations, and invite each child to select one.
4. Ask the children to form a line. Explain that when you say "insects fly," the children should toss their insects as far as they can.
5. After the children toss their insects, ask the children to find their insects and stand where they landed. Ask the children to describe how their bugs flew.
6. Line up all the children behind you. Have them hold their insects high above their heads and then follow you, making their insects "fly," as you run about the large open area with the children trailing behind you.

ASSESSMENT

Consider the following:
● Can the children tell you what affected the distances their insects could "fly"?
● Can the children describe their insects and count the number of sections the insects' bodies have?

Children's Books

Bees, Wasps, and Ants by George S. Fichter

The Best Bug Parade by Stuart Murphy

Monster Bugs by Lucille Recht Penner

Mary J. Murray, Mazomanie, WI

Butterfly Match

LEARNING OBJECTIVES

The children will:
1. Describe butterflies.
2. Match identical butterflies.

Materials

file folder
plastic or paper
   cutout butterflies
color copier or
   camera
glue stick
child-safe scissors

VOCABULARY

butterfly   match   pair   wings

PREPARATION

- Find an inexpensive set of plastic butterflies or paper cutouts of butterflies. Make color photocopies of them or take pictures.
- Create a file-folder activity with the copies of pictures glued to the inside of the file folder.

WHAT TO DO

1. Talk with the children about butterflies. Ask the children to describe butterflies they have seen.
2. Set out the file folder and plastic butterflies where the children have access to them.
3. Show the children each butterfly, and ask the children to describe the butterflies.
4. Explain that there are matching images of these butterflies in the file folder.
5. Challenge the children to work independently to match the loose butterflies to their pairs in the file folder.

TEACHER-TO-TEACHER TIP

- You can find inexpensive butterflies at craft stores.

ASSESSMENT

Consider the following:
- Can the children accurately describe the characteristics of butterflies?
- Can the children pair the plastic butterflies to their matching copies in the file folder?

Children's Books

Charlie the Caterpillar by Dom Deluise
From Caterpillar to Butterfly by Deborah Heiligman
Monarch Butterfly by Gail Gibbons
The Very Hungry Caterpillar by Eric Carle

Jackie Wright, Enid, OK

Taking Bees to the Flowers 3+

LEARNING OBJECTIVES

The children will:
1. Develop their small motor skills.
2. Learn about bees.
3. Practice following instructions.
4. Practice identifying colors.

Materials

selection of tweezers and tongs of different sizes

small ready-made bees or small yellow pompoms and permanent black marker

tweezers and small tongs in various sizes

artificial flowers

florist's foam or block of styrofoam

VOCABULARY

bee   flowers   pollen   tongs   tweezers

PREPARATION

- If you don't have small toy bees, make tiny, fluffy bees by drawing a stripe on small yellow pompoms with a permanent black marker.
- Set out the flowers in the block of foam.

WHAT TO DO

1. Use a selection of tweezers and tongs of different sizes, as appropriate to each child.
2. Tell the children that bees gather pollen from flowers.
3. Challenge the children to pick up bees with tweezers or tongs and transport them to the middle of each flower.
4. Younger children can use their fingers instead of tweezers. The distance between the bees and the flowers should vary according to the age of the children.

TEACHER-TO-TEACHER TIP

- You could combine this with a color exercise by asking the child to put a bee only on, say, a red or yellow flower.

POEM

Here Is a Beehive Traditional

Here is the beehive, where are the bees?   *One, two, three, four, five.*
Hidden away where nobody sees.   *Buzz, buzz, buzz.*
Watch and you will see them come out of their hives;

Children's Books

Beekeepers by Linda Oatman High
The Bee Tree by Patricia Polacco
Belinda Bee's Busy Year by Rusty Wise

ASSESSMENT

Consider the following:
- Ask the children where the bees go to collect their food.
- Can the children manage to use the tweezers or tongs to pick up the bees?
- Do the children choose the correct color if asked?

Anne Adeney, Plymouth, United Kingdom

Butterfly Bonanza

LEARNING OBJECTIVES

The children will:
1. Learn the names of colors.
2. Count objects.
3. Compare the sizes of different objects.
4. Compare groups of objects.

Materials

colored tissue
   paper
scissors (adult use
   only)
plastic tub
images of
   butterflies
paper plate
3' × 3' section of
   white mural
   paper

VOCABULARY

big   butterfly   color   count   fly   small

PREPARATION

● Cut a large number of 2" and 4" squares from the colored tissue paper.
● Twist each square in the center, creating a "butterfly" shape.
● Gently place all the butterflies in a large plastic tub.

WHAT TO DO

1. Gather the children together on the floor.
2. Talk with the children about butterflies. Show the children images of butterflies and ask them to describe what they see.
3. Use a plate to scoop a collection of butterflies from the tub and fling the butterflies over the heads of the children, inviting the children to catch one butterfly each.
4. Ask the children to form a large circle. Display the white mural paper in the center of the circle.
5. Invite each child to display and describe her butterfly and then lay it on the paper.
6. Toss several more scoops of butterflies onto the paper as the children watch them fly and land on the paper.
7. Invite one or two children to sort the butterflies into piles according to color or size, and then compare the number of butterflies in each pile.
8. Gently pick up the paper (with the butterflies inside) and roll it into a cone shape.
9. Then unroll the paper and let the butterflies again "fly" over the heads of the children.

ASSESSMENT

Consider the following:
● Can the children group the butterflies by size and color?
● Can the children count how many of a particular kind of butterfly there are?

Children's Books

Butterfly Express by
Jane Belk Moncure
*Flying Colors; Butterflies
in Your Backyard* by
Nancy Loewen
*The Very Hungry
Caterpillar* by Eric Carle

Mary J. Murray, Mazomanie, WI

Find the Bugs

3+

LEARNING OBJECTIVES

The children will:
1. Recognize insects and bugs.
2. Develop their small motor skills.

small baskets
plastic bugs (bees,
  ants, spiders,
  ladybugs,
  butterflies, and
  so on)
buttons
beads

VOCABULARY

| ant | bug | insect | spider |
| bee | butterfly | ladybug | |

PREPARATION

● Place the plastic bugs, buttons, and beads in the baskets. **Safety Note:** Be sure to supervise carefully.

WHAT TO DO

1. Ask the children what kinds of bugs they see in their neighborhoods. Ask the children what the bugs look like.
2. Give each child a basket filled with plastic bugs, buttons, and beads.
3. Have the children find all of the bugs in their baskets.
4. Once the children have found all of the bugs in their baskets, challenge them to sort the bugs by type. Help the children name the bugs, if needed.

Children's Books

The Best Book of Bugs by Claire Llewellyn
Bugs! Bugs! Bugs! by Bob Barner
My Bug Book by Melissa Stewart
My First Book of Bugs and Spiders by Ticktock Media, Ltd.

POEM

Bloomin' Bugs by Laura Wynkoop

Butterflies flutter,   *The bug world awakens*
And bumblebees zoom.   *When spring is in bloom!*

ASSESSMENT

Consider the following:
● Display two of the plastic bugs. Can the children name them?
● Can the children sort the plastic bugs from the rest of the objects in the baskets?

Laura Wynkoop, San Dimas, CA

I Love Honey

4+

LEARNING OBJECTIVES

The children will:
1. Work with numbers 1–5.
2. Read number words from "one" to "five."

Materials

marker
tagboard
scissors
markers
pocket chart
(optional)

VOCABULARY

bee	hive	pollen
flower	honey	

PREPARATION

- Make two sets of cards. Make one set shaped like bees; cut out a total of 30. Make the second set shaped like beehives; cut out a total of 10. On the beehive set, copy a number from 1 to 5 on five of the beehives, and write number words "one" through "five" on the other five.

WHAT TO DO

1. Talk with the children about bees. Ask the children to describe what they have seen bees doing.
2. Explain to the children that bees are out gathering pollen from flowers and bringing it back to their hives to make honey.
3. Show the children the bee and beehive cutouts, and explain that for this game, certain beehives need a specific number of bees to bring them nectar.
4. Challenge the children to match the correct number of bee cutouts to each hive.

TEACHER-TO-TEACHER TIP

- Use a pocket chart, if available. Laminate both sets of cards for durability.
- For children who have difficulty counting, consider tracing the correct number of bee cutouts on the beehives so the children can match the correct number of bees to the hive.

ASSESSMENT

Consider the following:
- Can the children correctly match the sets to the numeral words?
- Can the children count aloud the number of bees that belong in each hive?

Jackie Wright, Enid, OK

Children's Books

The Bee-Man of Orn by Frank R. Stockton
Buzz Said the Bee by Wendy Cheyette Lewison
The Honeybee and the Robber by Eric Carle
Honeybees by Jane Lecht

Insect Shoe Patterns

LEARNING OBJECTIVES

The children will:
1. Make a pattern.
2. Develop their small motor skills.
3. Learn to count to six.

Materials

baby shoes (or the
   children's shoes)
empty wrapping
   paper rolls
scissors (adult use
   only)
thick string
images of insects
   where all legs are
   visible

VOCABULARY

insect   left   pattern   right   six

PREPARATION

- Make several "insects" using sections of wrapping paper rolls for their bodies and string for their legs.
- Collect several matching shoes. Place left shoes on one side of the insect and right shoes on the other.

WHAT TO DO

1. Talk with the children about insects. Show the children images of insects and invite them to count the feet they see. Explain that all insects have six legs and therefore have six feet.
2. Set out the "insect" and show the children its six legs and feet.
3. Challenge the children to make a pattern with the shoes on the insect's right feet and then to match the pattern on the insect's left feet.

POEM

Quick Little Insect by Kristen Peters

A little insect is very fast.
Don't blink your eyes; he'll run right past.
With tiny legs that run in sync.

He'll be gone before you blink.
His movement is a constant flow.
Here's his head and here's his toe!

TEACHER-TO-TEACHER TIP

- Make your own insect images using different-colored ink pads. Have the children draw the body and then use thumbprints to make the insect's six legs.

ASSESSMENT

Consider the following:
- Do the children understand how many legs an insect has?
- Are the children able to create the correct pattern with the shoes?

Children's Books

The Best Book of Bugs
   by Claire Llewellyn
More Bugs in Boxes by
   David A. Carter
Pattern Bugs by
   Trudy Harris

Kristen Peters, Mattituck, NY

Let Your Fingers Do the Sizing

4+

LEARNING OBJECTIVES

The children will:
1. Sort items according to relative size: small, medium, and large.
2. Learn about the different sizes of various insects.

Materials

egg cartons
scissors (adult use only)
glue
wiggle eyes in assorted sizes
pipe cleaners
tissue paper in assorted colors
various small, medium, and large versions of different objects

VOCABULARY

insect   large   medium   small   wings

PREPARATION

- Cut the bottoms of egg cartons into two-bump sections, three-bump sections, and four-bump sections. Poke holes in the center of the bugs.
- Cut pipe cleaners to 5" lengths and cut tissue paper into 4" × 1½" rectangles.

WHAT TO DO

1. Show the children images of bugs of various sizes. Explain that some bugs are very small, while some can be quite large.
2. Give each child one of each of the three sizes of insect "bodies" (egg-carton cutouts).
3. Help the children pick out tissue paper for wings and secure it to the bug by folding a pipe cleaner in a "U" shape across the middle of the tissue paper, poking the pipe cleaner ends through the hole in the bug, and twisting the pipe cleaner together on the underside of the bug.
4. When all three types of bugs have wings, help the children glue wiggle eyes to the bugs.
5. Challenge the children to line their "insects" up by size.
6. Ask the children to hold up a particular size of insect. Ask the children to imagine what that insect does all day. Listen to their responses.
7. Repeat with the other egg-carton insects.
8. Challenge the children to count the total number of body sections the insects have.
9. Set out various small, medium, and large groups of objects. Challenge the children to match these objects to the correct insects in their sets.

ASSESSMENT

Consider the following:
- Can the children distinguish between the small, medium, and large egg-carton insects?
- Can the children match other objects to the correct insects, according to size?

Children's Books

Bugs Are Best! by Ruth Thomas
The Icky Bug Alphabet Book by Jerry Pallotta
The Very Hungry Caterpillar by Eric Carle

Susan Oldham Hill, Lakeland, FL

Measuring with Caterpillars 4+

LEARNING OBJECTIVES

The children will:

1. Improve their counting skills.
2. Improve their measuring and comparing skills.
3. Develop their oral language skills.
4. Begin to differentiate by length.

Materials

chenille stems in
   assorted colors
pencil
plastic bin or
   shoebox
small plastic
   container
common objects to
   measure, such as
   a pencil, ruler,
   crayon, book,
   and so on
images of
   caterpillars

VOCABULARY

caterpillars   count   long   numbers   short

PREPARATION

- Create fuzzy caterpillar manipulatives by wrapping each chenille stem tightly around a pencil to create 2″ coiled caterpillar shapes.
- Place the assorted caterpillars in the plastic container and set it in the box along with the common objects.

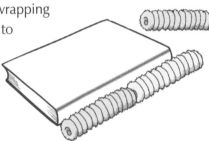

WHAT TO DO

1. Show the children images of caterpillars, and engage them in a discussion about what they see. Talk about how long caterpillars are, and ask if they think they could measure something by comparing it to a caterpillar. You might even want to start a discussion about inchworms and why they are called that.
2. Place the box in the math center.
3. Demonstrate how to measure each item by laying a row of caterpillars along the length of each object. **Note:** Explain to the children that they should not use real caterpillars to attempt to measure objects.
4. Invite the children to count how many caterpillars long each item is.
5. Encourage the children to compare the lengths of the objects by making statements such as "The pencil is longer than the crayon." "The book is longer than the ruler."
6. Have the children return the materials to the box so the activity is ready for the next person.

ASSESSMENT

Consider the following:

- Can the children count how many caterpillars it takes to measure an object?
- Do the children understand the basic concept of measurement?

Mary J. Murray, Mazomanie, WI

Children's Books

The Bug Guy: 10 Words by Sean Groathouse
Caterpillars, Bugs and Butterflies by Mel Boring
The Very Hungry Caterpillar by Eric Carle
What's That Sound Wooly Bear? by Philemon Sturges

Shape Bugs

4+

LEARNING OBJECTIVES

The children will:
1. Learn various insect names.
2. Learn different shapes.

scissors (adult use
  only)
glue
construction paper
pictures of insects

VOCABULARY

circle	insect names	shape	triangle
insect	rectangle	square	

PREPARATION

- Cut out several different shapes from the construction paper.
- Cut some that are very small and some that are larger.
- Make sure to cut out ovals, circles, rectangles, and triangles.
- Ahead of time, make some examples of shape-built insects for the children to look at.

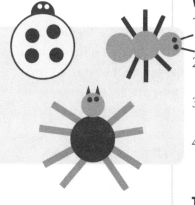

WHAT TO DO

1. Set out pictures of actual insects. Ask the children to identify those insects, and then describe how they look.
2. Show the children the examples you made that correspond to the insects they were just discussing.
3. Show the children how to assemble different insects with the shapes that you have already cut out.
4. To make a more realistic bug, use a larger shape for the body. The smaller shapes can make up the legs, head, and other bug body parts.

TEACHER-toTEACHER TIP

- You can assemble different insects beforehand as an example. For instance, a large oval with small circles and thin rectangles could be assembled to look like a ladybug. You can also explain to them how many legs insects have, what antennae are, and so on.

Children's Books

The Best Bug Parade by
  Stuart Murphy
Big Bugs by
  Mary Gribbin
Bugs! by
  David Greenberg

ASSESSMENT

Consider the following:
- Can the children identify the individual names of the shapes they are using?
- Can the children say which insects they are creating using the shapes?

Hilary Romig, Las Cruces, NM

Bug Races

LEARNING OBJECTIVES

The children will:

1. Learn about various types of bugs.
2. Familiarize themselves with the concept of graphing.

VOCABULARY

bug	graph	measure	results
compare	insect	race	

WHAT TO DO

1. Spread out different pictures of various bugs. Discuss the bugs' life cycles, diet, and so on. Talk about the way the bugs get from one place to another: crawling, flying, hopping.
2. Tell the children they are going to have a bug race.
3. On large paper, create a graph by gluing the various bug pictures across the bottom and then adding numbers up the left side ranging from 1 to 100.
4. Glue bug cutouts to match the pictures on small toy cars (one per child) and write one child's name on each bug.
5. Place tape for the starting line on the floor and tape for the finish line at a distance.
6. Have the children come up two at a time to race their bugs.
7. Let them use yardsticks to measure how far their bugs traveled.
8. Help them graph their results by their bug picture on the chart.
9. Afterward, ask the children which type of bug might win a real race: one that crawls, flies, or hops?

ASSESSMENT

Consider the following:

- Can the children identify various insects by their characteristics?
- Can the children tell you how certain bugs get from place to place?
- Do the children indicate a basic understanding of graphing?

Lisa Chichester, Parkersburg, WV

Materials

miniature cars
pictures of different
  kinds of bugs
large paper
crayons
small bug cutouts
  (that match the
  pictures of the
  bugs)
tape
yardsticks

Children's Books

The Best Bug Parade by
  Stuart Murphy
Big Bugs by
  Mary Gribbin
Bugs! by
  David Greenberg

Counting Caterpillar Puzzle

LEARNING OBJECTIVES

The children will:
1. Learn how to make puzzles.
2. Develop their small motor skills.

Materials

images of
   caterpillars
books about
   caterpillars (see
   list below)
paper
2 pieces of heavy
   corrugated
   cardboard
   (9″ × 12″ or
   larger)
glue
utility knife (adult
   use only)
felt-tip pen

VOCABULARY

base	butterfly	cutout	legs	piece
body	caterpillar	head	numbers	puzzle

PREPARATION

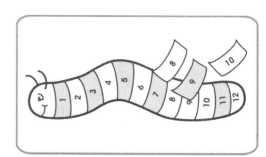

- Draw a caterpillar and divide it into 12 puzzle-piece shapes. Number the pieces 1–12.
- Glue the drawing to one of the pieces of cardboard.
- Use a utility knife to cut the caterpillar out of the cardboard (adult-only step). Glue the remaining frame of the caterpillar to the second piece of cardboard.
- Cut the caterpillar into its 12 labeled sections. Fit each piece into the puzzle, tracing its outline into the base of the puzzle as you go.
- In the spaces you just traced on the base, write the number names that correspond to the numerals on their matching pieces.

WHAT TO DO

1. Engage the children in a conversation about caterpillars. Show the children the images of caterpillars and ask the children to talk about what they see: head, body, legs, and so on.
2. Read the children a book about caterpillars.
3. Show the children the puzzle and encourage them to explore the pieces and read the numerals and number names.
4. The children can work together to put the puzzle together.

ASSESSMENT

Consider the following:
- Ask the children what they learned about caterpillars.
- Are the children able to put the puzzle together?

Children's Books

Charlie the Caterpillar by Dom Deluise
Clara Caterpillar by Pamela Duncan Edwards
The Very Hungry Caterpillar by Eric Carle

Cookie Zingarelli, Columbus, OH

Let's Count the Legs

LEARNING OBJECTIVES

The children will:
1. Practice counting.
2. Develop an understanding of the idea of comparison.

Materials

pictures of insects
    and spiders with
    all their legs
    visible
2 bowls

VOCABULARY

ant	bug	fly	leg
arachnid	butterfly	grasshopper	
bee	cricket	insect	

PREPARATION

- Find pictures of insects and spiders in old books or magazines.
- Make two color copies of the images. Attach one copy to the wall for the children to use as reference.
- Cut the legs from the images of the insects and spiders, and laminate the bodies and legs. Place the bodies in one bowl and the legs in another bowl to keep things orderly for the children.

WHAT TO DO

1. Set out the bowls of insect and spider bodies and legs and show the children the whole images of insects and spiders on the wall.
2. Engage the children in a discussion about spiders and insects, asking the children to describe various characteristics of each.
3. Explain to the children that insects have six legs, while spiders have eight legs.
4. Show the children the images of spiders and insects on the wall, and count the number of legs each creature has.
5. Invite the children to sort through the bowls of bodies and legs and to try to match the legs to the bodies. Encourage the children to use the complete images on the wall as models.

SONG

- Sing "The Ants Go Marching" with the children.

ASSESSMENT

Consider the following:
- Do the children understand the difference between insects and spiders?
- Can the children count the number of legs on each creature?
- Can the children match the correct sets of legs to the correct creatures?

Children's Books

Bugs Are Best! by
    Ruth Thomas
Bugs Are Insects by
    Anne Rockwell
Bugs Up Close by
    Diane Swanson

Eileen Lucas, Fort McMurray, Alberta, Canada

Six Legs

5+

Materials

insect pictures
clay

LEARNING OBJECTIVES

The children will:
1. Develop their counting skills.
2. Develop their small motor skills.

VOCABULARY

count	insect	six
group	leg	

WHAT TO DO

1. Show the children images of insects and ask them to count the number of legs they see.
2. Ask the children how many legs they have, and have them imagine what it would be like to walk with six legs. That would be a lot of shoes to put on every morning!
3. Tell the children they will be making a clay insect. Take some clay and roll a ball about $1\frac{1}{2}''$ in diameter. This will be one part of an insect.
4. Roll a smaller quantity of clay between your fingers to form a cylinder about $1'' \times \frac{1}{8}''$. This will be one of the insect's six legs.
5. Roll two more legs in this manner and press the three legs against one side of the larger ball.
6. Form another three legs and press these against the other side of the ball, so you have an insect with six legs. Count the legs with the children.
7. Separate the children into groups of six and have each child in the group make her own insect.
8. When the children finish making their insects, ask the children to place them in a row and count the total number of legs on all the insects in their group.

ASSESSMENT

Consider the following:
- How many insect legs can the children count?
- Do the children understand that insects have six legs?

Patrick Mitchell, Yagoto, Nagoya, Japan

Children's Books

The Best Bug Parade by Stuart Murphy
Bugs! by David Greenberg
One Hundred Shoes by Charles Ghigna
Pattern Bugs by Trudy Harris

Chirp, Cricket, Chirp!

4+

LEARNING OBJECTIVES

The children will:

1. Learn how crickets make noise and communicate through stridulation, which is the chirping sound crickets make by rubbing body parts together.
2. Develop their small motor skills.

Materials

plastic comb (1 per child)
Popsicle™ stick (1 per child)
ridged rhythm sticks (1 pair per child; optional)

VOCABULARY

bug	stridulation (rubbing one	wings
insect	body part against another,	
legs	such as wings and legs, to	
	make a sound)	

WHAT TO DO

1. Talk with the children about the sound crickets make. Male crickets rub their wings together to make a chirping sound. When done softly, the chirp attracts females. When done aggressively, the chirp is meant to scare away intruders and serve as a warning. In this exercise, the children will learn about the nonverbal communication that occurs between crickets, and about the mechanics of "stridulation."
2. Have the children rub their Popsicle sticks against the teeth of their comb to produce a "cricket" sound. They can practice making soft and hard sounds to mimic cricket chirps.
3. Have the children guess if the sounds are "angry" or "friendly" and see if they can decode what a cricket might be trying to say when they make these sounds.
4. For more fun, play music in the background and encourage the children to jump like crickets as they play their comb instruments.
5. Challenge the children to think of ways they communicate with one another nonverbally.

TEACHER-TO-TEACHER TIP

- Recordings of actual cricket chirps can be downloaded from the Internet and played for the children as an example.

ASSESSMENT

Consider the following:

- Can the children think of ways that they communicate with one another nonverbally?
- Can the children tell you how a cricket makes noise?

Monica Shaughnessy, Katy, TX

Children's Books

Chirp, Chirp!: Crickets in Your Backyard by Nancy Loewen
Crickets and Grasshoppers by Ann O. Squire
The Very Quiet Cricket by Eric Carle

Pollinators

4+

LEARNING OBJECTIVES

The children will:
1. Play an outdoor game that illustrates how insects pollinate flowers and trees.
2. Develop their large motor skills.

Materials

colored balls
at least one container (box, bin, or pail) for each color of ball used

VOCABULARY

bee	pollen	predator
flower	pollinate	

PREPARATION

- Place all the balls that are the same color into one container.
- Place the ball containers randomly around the playing area.

WHAT TO DO

1. Discuss the terms "pollen" and "pollination" with the children. Highlight how important pollination is to the production of fruits and vegetables. Discuss how insects like bees and butterflies help the process of pollination. Explain that birds are natural predators for insects like bees and butterflies.
2. Explain to the children that the playing area is a field of flowers waiting to be pollinated. Each box represents a flower, and each ball is a bit of pollen from that flower.
3. Most of the children will be pollinators. For every five or six pollinators, assign one child to be a bird.
4. To play, the pollinators run between the containers. At each container, they drop off the ball they picked up at the previous container and pick up a new ball.
5. The birds try to tag the pollinators. If a bird tags a pollinator, that pollinator is out of the game and must sit on the sideline.
6. Play concludes when time is up or all of the pollinators have been tagged.
7. At the end of the game, take time to observe how the colored balls are distributed in the play area. Ask the children to raise their hands if they think the field has been pollinated well.

ASSESSMENT

Consider the following:
- Are the children beginning to understand the importance of pollination? Can they describe what pollination is?
- Can the children work together to "pollinate" the field?

Janet Hammond, Mount Laurel, NJ

Children's Books

The Bee-Man of Orn by Frank R. Stockton
Buzz Said the Bee by Wendy Cheyette Lewison
The Honey Bee and the Robber by Eric Carle

Bottles of Bugs

3+

LEARNING OBJECTIVES

The children will:
1. Identify various bugs.
2. Identify color.
3. Develop their counting skills.
4. Learn to follow directions.

Materials

5 or more large
clear plastic
water bottles or
other wide
mouth bottles
(20 oz. or larger)
assortment of small
plastic toy insects

VOCABULARY

bottle   bugs   colors   count   insects

PREPARATION

● Place an assortment of insects inside each plastic bottle and close the lid tightly.

WHAT TO DO

1. Display the bottles of bugs in a prominent place in the classroom.
2. Each day select five children to take a bottle to their resting mat.
3. Invite the children to lie on their backs and look at the bugs through the plastic bottle, rotating it as they peek at the various bugs moving about.

MORE TO DO

● After rest time, ask a child to describe what she sees as she observes the bugs in the bottle. Have the children answer questions about the colors, shapes, sizes, number, and types of insects they see.
● Invite the children to trace around a bottle on a sheet of paper and then add insect stickers to the drawing. Invite the children to teach a partner about the insects inside their bottle.

TEACHER-TO-TEACHER TIPS

● Instead of plastic insects, attach insect stickers to both sides of very small pieces of tagboard. Place the tagboard insect cards inside the bottles.
● If some children fall asleep, be sure to allow time for them to observe the bugs in a bottle later in the day.

Children's Books

Beetle Bop by
Denise Fleming
Beetles by Edana Eckart
Bug Safari by
Bob Barner
Have You Seen Bugs?
by Joanne Oppenheim

ASSESSMENT

Consider the following:
● Can the children identify the colors of the various insects in the bottle?
● Can the children describe the insects in the bottle?

Mary J. Murray, Mazomanie, WI

Snuggle with a Bug

3+

LEARNING OBJECTIVES

The children will:
1. Rest quietly.
2. Improve their vocabulary.
3. Develop their ability to follow directions.

Materials

assortment of beanbag pal insects
colorful fabric squares (for insect blankets)
butterfly net

VOCABULARY

insect   quiet   rest   sleep

PREPARATION

- Display the beanbag insect toys in a basket.
- Display the small insect blankets in a pile next to the basket.

WHAT TO DO

1. Teach the children the following song:

   Twinkle, Twinkle, Little Bug by Mary J. Murray
   (Tune: "Twinkle, Twinkle, Little Star")

   Twinkle, twinkle, little bug,   *I'll hold you and hug you tight.*
   You're so cute and fun to love.   *Twinkle, twinkle, little bug,*
   Time for rest, day or night.   *You're so cute and fun to love.*

2. Just before rest time, invite the children to sing this song softly.
3. Move around the classroom with the butterfly net, touching the net on each child's shoulder, signaling that child to go up and select an insect friend to snuggle with during rest time.
4. Have each child quietly take one insect and one insect blanket, and carry them to his resting place.
5. The song continues until every child is resting with an insect friend.
6. After rest time, invite the children to whisper their thoughts about their insect, and then return the insects and the blankets to the basket.

ASSESSMENT

Consider the following:
- Are the children able to recite the song from memory?
- Do the children choose different insects and blankets, or do they have individual ones to which they are partial?
- How well do the children wait for their turns to pick their insect pals?

Children's Books

Beginning Fun with Bugs and Butterflies by Gayle Bittinger
Bugs by James E. Gerholdt
The Very Lonely Firefly by Eric Carle

Mary J. Murray, Mazomanie, WI

Bug Hunt

4+

LEARNING OBJECTIVES

The children will:

1. Develop their small motor skills.
2. Practice counting.
3. Enjoy a sensory/exploratory experience.

Materials

water table or large
   rectangular tray
   filled with sand
   or cornmeal
selection of plastic
   bugs
paper cup for each
   child

VOCABULARY

capture	find	insect names
count	hunt	search

PREPARATION

- Hide the bugs in the sand and water table prior to the activity.

WHAT TO DO

1. Show the children some samples of the various plastic bugs you have hidden around the classroom. Help the children identify the bugs by name, and discuss their various characteristics.
2. Divide the children into groups of three or four.
3. Enable each group to have a turn to hunt for bugs and collect them in their cups.
4. Encourage the children to count the bugs in their cups at the end of the activity.
5. Praise their efforts and prompt them to bury the bugs for the next group.

TEACHER-TO-TEACHER TIP

- Caution the children not to put the bugs in their mouths.

ASSESSMENT

Consider the following:

- How well do the children work together in groups?
- Make a chart to record the results of the activity to post or file. Example:

I	Found	The	Bugs!
Jason	found	4	bugs!
Lourdes	found	7	bugs!

Children's Books

The Bugliest Bug by
Carol Diggory Shields
Bugs! Bugs! Bugs! by
Bob Barner
I Love Bugs! by
Philemon Sturges

Susan Sharkey, Fletcher Hills, CA

Entomologist of the Day

4+

LEARNING OBJECTIVES

The children will:
1. Develop role playing skills.
2. Identify insects.

Materials

10 plastic toy insects
(or pictures of
insects)
word card that reads
"entomologist"
plastic bin or bucket
with a handle
magnifying glass
small plastic animal
cage or bug
catcher
list of the insect
names printed on
a 4" × 6" note
card
insect-identification
handbook
hat and shirt

Children's Books

Amazing Bugs by
Miranda MacQuitty
The Best Bug Parade by
Stuart Murphy
Bugs! by
David Greenberg
*Caterpillars, Bugs, and
Butterflies* by
Mel Boring

VOCABULARY

binoculars   find   magnifying glass
entomology   insects

PREPARATION

- Display 10 toy insects around the classroom.
- Place the container of materials in a select place in the classroom, near the shirt and hat.
- Display the "Entomologist" word card near the materials.
- Glue several small bugs to a fabric cap and shirt to create an entomologist's hat and lab coat.

WHAT TO DO

1. Write the words "entomology" and "entomologist" on the chalk board. Explain that entomology is the study of insects and that a person who studies insects is an "entomologist."
2. Each day, choose a child to be the "Entomologist of the Day."
3. Explain to all the children that there are several insects living in the classroom and invite them to search around the room for insects.
4. When they find an insect, have the children call the entomologist of the day over so the entomologist can place the insect in the bug catcher. Help the entomologist identify the name of the insect on the list of bugs.
5. Model how an entomologist might study each insect: observe it with the magnifying glass, read about it in the insect handbook.
6. After the children find all 10 insects, go to a table, spill out the bugs, and challenge the children to name each insect aloud.

ASSESSMENT

Consider the following:
- Do the children understand what an "entomologist" is?
- Can the children identify the insects?

Mary J. Murray, Mazomanie, WI

Is It an Insect?

LEARNING OBJECTIVES

The children will:
1. Identify insects based upon the number of legs.
2. Group insects and other animals into two categories.

Materials

toy insects and
    animals
place to classify
    each group of
    toys
packets of pictures
    of insects and
    animals for each
    child
construction paper
    for each child
glue sticks

VOCABULARY

body	insect	six
bug	legs	

PREPARATION

● Gather the pictures and toy insects and animals. Fold each piece of construction paper and label one half "Insects" and the other half "Other Animals."

WHAT TO DO

1. Explain that insects are animals, but many animals are not insects. Insects have six legs. Count the legs on animals together to decide which are insects.
2. Pass out the toy bugs and animals, or pictures of insects and animals. Ask the children to study these and decide whether they are insects.
3. Explain that you will classify them into two categories and define these.
4. Demonstrate how to do this by classifying one insect and one animal for the children. Have the children classify their toys individually. The rest of the class can help decide if the classification is correct.
5. When everyone has had a turn, give each child a packet of pictures and a construction paper chart. Assist them while they glue the pictures into the correct locations.

TEACHER-TO-TEACHER TIP

● Be careful to use pictures of adult insects, not larval stages.

ASSESSMENT

Consider the following:
● Can the children count the numbers of legs insects on the insects and other animals?
● Do the children classify the pictures correctly?

Children's Books

The Grouchy Ladybug
    by Eric Carle
The Very Busy Spider by
    Eric Carle
*The Very Hungry
Caterpillar* by Eric Carle

Debbie Vilardi, Commack, NY

Spider Webs

LEARNING OBJECTIVES

The children will:
1. Improve eye-hand coordination.
2. Develop their small motor skills.

Materials

paper plates
hole punch
scissors (adult use
   only)
black yarn
black construction
   paper
plastic toy spider

VOCABULARY

home   spider   weave   web

PREPARATION
● Cut several lengths of yarn in lengths between 3'–5'.

WHAT TO DO
1. Talk with the children about spiders, specifically about the webs they live in. Explain that spiders use their webs both to live in as well as catch food. Ask the children to describe how they think spiders make their webs.
2. Explain that the children will be making model spider webs today.
3. Set out the materials for the children.
4. Model for the children how to punch holes around the outside edge of a plate. Help those children who have difficulty with this part of the activity.
5. Help the children knot one end of a length of yarn to one hole, and then model how to string the yarn through the holes so that a web-form begins to appear.
6. Observe as the children create their webs. Encourage the children to make their own unique patterns.
7. When the children's lengths of yarn are almost completely used, help the children knot a plastic toy spider to the end, and then tie the spider somewhere on the web.

TEACHER-TO-TEACHER TIP
● Wrap masking tape around the loose end of the yarn to prevent it from fraying and make it easier for the children to push it through the holes.

ASSESSMENT
Consider the following:
● Do the children understand what uses spiders have for their webs?
● Can the children create their own webs independently?

Children's Books

Aaaarrgghh, Spider! by
   Lydia Monk
The Itsy Bitsy Spider by
   Iza Trapani
Little Miss Spider by
   David Kirk
Time For Kids: Spiders!
   by the Editors of
   Time For Kids
The Very Busy Spider by
   Eric Carle

Sandra Ryan, Buffalo, NY

Mason Bee Houses

LEARNING OBJECTIVES

The children will:
1. Recognize a mason bee versus a honeybee.
2. Learn to appreciate beneficial insects.

Materials

paper straws
(plastic may
contaminate the
bee eggs with
bacteria)
glue
scissors (adult use
only)
waxed cardboard
single-serving
milk or juice
cartons
hammer
long nails
pictures of honey-
bees and orchard
mason bees

VOCABULARY

bee   hive   mason   nest   pollen

PREPARATION

- Cut paper straws in half, and then vary the length of each slightly (mason bees prefer this kind of pattern).
- Cut a carton a little bit longer than the straw halves so they fit inside with a little overhang to protect from the weather.

WHAT TO DO

1. Show the children pictures of honeybees and orchard mason bees and discuss the differences between them (size, color).
2. Help the children spread a thin layer of glue on the inside bottom of the cardboard carton, place the straw halves in until full.
3. As the children do this, talk with them about mason bees. Explain that mason bees are solitary, unlike social honeybees. They have no hive to defend nor do they make honey. Their sting is similar to a mosquito bite and they only sting if pinched. Like honeybees, mason bees are helpful because they spread pollen and help fruits and vegetables develop. Mason bees lay eggs in holes that beetles chew in trees, similar to the shapes of the straws the children are placing in the cartons. After laying their eggs, the bees close up the holes with mud.

4. Take the children outside and put up the bee houses in designated spots.
5. With the children, check the bee houses throughout the spring and early summer to see if any mason bees are using them. Dispose of the houses in the winter.

ASSESSMENT

Consider the following:
- Do the children understand the importance of pollinating insects?
- Do the children recognize both honeybees and orchard mason bees?

Children's Books

The Bee-Man of Orn by
Frank R. Stockton
Buzz Said the Bee by
Wendy Cheyette
Lewison
*The Honey Bee and the
Robber* by Eric Carle

Kay Flowers, Summerfield, OH

Honey Milk Balls

3+

LEARNING OBJECTIVES

The children will:

1. Learn to follow directions.
2. Learn about recipes.
3. Learn that bees make honey, which is a tasty food.

Materials

mixing bowls
Note: Ensure that no children have allergies to the ingredients before proceeding with this activity.

Ingredients

- ¼ cup honey
- ½ cup peanut butter
- 1 cup non-fat powdered milk
- 1 cup shredded coconut
- 1 cup uncooked rolled oats or ½ cup graham cracker crumbs

WHAT TO DO

1. Talk with the children about honey, about what a tasty treat it is. Explain to the children that honey comes from bees.
2. With the children, mix the first four ingredients well, and then knead by hand until blended.
3. Shape this mixture into 1" balls.
4. Roll the honey milk balls in coconut. This should make two dozen.
5. Enjoy the snack together.

MORE TO DO

- Add apples: Cut the number of apples you wish to use into slices. Place on a plate with individual cups of honey for each person. Just dip the apples into the honey and eat. This is a special treat during the Jewish High Holy Days.

POEM

Five Little Flowers by Cookie Zingarelli

Five little flowers
Planted in the garden.
A long came _____,

And picked one flower,
Now there are four.
(insert a child's name)

Repeat the verse, reducing the number of flowers until there are none.

ASSESSMENT

Consider the following:

- Are the children able to work together and follow the recipe to make the honey milk balls?
- Do the children indicate an understanding that honey comes from bees?

Children's Books

The Big Honey Hunt by Stan and Jan Berenstain
Honeybee's Busy Day by Richard Fowler
My World: Bees by Christine Butterworth
A Taste of Honey by Nancy Elizabeth Wallace

Cookie Zingarelli, Columbus, OH

Baking Ladybug Cookies

4+

LEARNING OBJECTIVES

The children will:
1. Learn how people prepare food.
2. Develop their small motor skills.

Materials

2 tablespoons
  water
2 bowls
2 wooden spoons
icing tube
weighing scales
oval or round
  cookie cutters
Note: This recipe
  makes about 30
  small cookies.

VOCABULARY

bake	cookie cutter	mix	spoon
bowl	ladybug	oven	

WHAT TO DO

Safety Note: Allow the children to do as much as they can, but using the oven is an adult-only part of this activity.

Ingredients

- 2½ cups flour
- 4 oz. margarine or butter
- 1 egg yolk
- ½ cup plus 2 tablespoons sugar
- 1 teaspoon vanilla extract
- 1¼ cups powered sugar
- red and black food coloring

1. Heat the oven to 325° F.
2. Let the children help make the cookies. Put the butter and sugar into your large mixing bowl, and mix with the wooden spoon. Add egg yolk and vanilla. Continue to mix. Add the flour until you have a dough-like consistency. Use hands to finish mixing the ingredients.
3. Roll out the cookie dough on a floured board until it is about ¼"–½".
4. Use cookie cutters to make ladybug body shapes. Put shapes on a baking tray and bake in the oven for 10–15 minutes at 375° (adult-only step).
5. Cool cookies on a rack (adult-only step).
6. Put 1 cup of powered sugar into a bowl and mix with water and a few drops of red food coloring. Add liquid slowly until you have desired consistency.
7. Mix ¼ cup of powered sugar with black food coloring and a small amount of water. When the cookies are cool, cover with red icing and leave it to set.
8. Using an icing tube, dot the black icing on for spots and eyes.
9. Have the children choose how many spots they want their Ladybug Cookie to have.

ASSESSMENT

Consider the following:
- Do the children understand the process of making food?
- How well are the children able to participate in the activity?

Jane Moran, Ludlow, United Kingdom

Children's Books

The Grouchy Ladybug by Eric Carle
Ladybug, Ladybug by Ruth Brown
Ten Little Ladybugs by Melanie Gerth and Laura Huliska-Beith

Butterfly Snack

4+

LEARNING OBJECTIVES

The children will:

1. Demonstrate the recognition of shapes by choosing the correct shape to go on the opposite wing (symmetry).
2. Develop their small motor skills.

Materials

finger sandwiches
pickles
pretzels
olives or raisins

VOCABULARY

butterfly	rectangle	symmetry
circle	square	triangle

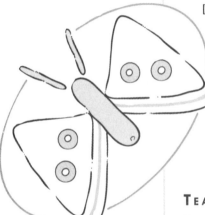

WHAT TO DO

1. Talk with the children about butterflies, and how they have symmetrical wings. Define "symmetry" for the children.
2. Explain that the children will be making and enjoying symmetrical snacks.
3. Cut finger sandwiches in triangle quarters.
4. Give each child two quarters of the sandwich for the wings, place a slice of pickle in the middle for the body and a pretzel stick broken into halves for antennas.
5. Consider using olives or raisins for spots.
6. Enjoy the snack!

TEACHER-TO-TEACHER TIP

- Make clothespin butterflies with the children: Fold small squares of tissue paper in half, put drops of food coloring in an eye-dropper. Drop colors on the tissue paper. Clip a clothespin in the middle. Add pipe cleaners for antennas. Draw a face. Each child has a butterfly with symmetrical wings.

SONG

Butterfly Wings by Kristen Peters

A butterfly has wings so light
To watch them fly is quite a sight.

They flutter and are fancy free
With details of shaped symmetry.

ASSESSMENT

Consider the following:

- Do the children understand the meaning of the word "symmetry"?
- Can the children create symmetrical snacks?

Kristen Peters, Mattituck, NY

Children's Books

The Butterfly Alphabet by Kjell B. Sandved
Good Night Sweet Butterflies by Dawn Bentley
Metamorphoses: Butterfly by Arthur John L' Hommedieu
Symmetry in Nature by Allyson Valentine Schrier

Spider Web Snacks

4+

LEARNING OBJECTIVES

The children will:
1. Prepare food.
2. Learn about spiders.
3. Develop their ability to follow directions.

Materials

rice cakes
2–3 cans of
  processed
  squeezable
  cheese
gummy fruit snacks
raisins or other small
  edibles such as
  sunflower seeds,
  dried fruit, or nuts
paper plates

VOCABULARY

bugs	eat	munch	web
crunch	insects	spider	

WHAT TO DO

1. Talk with the children about spiders and spider webs or read one of the spider books listed on this page, and then gather the children around for this fun snack activity.
2. Provide each child with a rice cake.
3. Guide each child as they squirt a spider web across their rice cake, using the bottle of squeezable cheese.
4. Provide the children with a piece of fruit snack to represent the "spider" and have them place it on the web of cheese.
5. Invite the children to add other little "bugs" (seeds, nuts, dried fruit pieces) to the spider web for the spider to eat.
6. After each child has prepared the snack, invite the children to munch away on this fun edible spider web.

TEACHER-TO-TEACHER TIPS

- Use graham crackers in place of rice cakes for a less expensive treat.
- Make a simple spider puppet by sewing felt eyes to a glove. Attach three more "legs" to the puppet by sewing three fingers cut from the other glove, to the puppet. Invite the children to manipulate this fun glove puppet as the children teach small groups of classmates what they know about spiders.

ASSESSMENT

Consider the following:
- Invite each child to talk about her spider web with a partner before they eat the snack.
- Display a picture of a spider in its web. Provide a child with a spider puppet. Allow the child to explain how a spider spins a web, catches its prey, and so on.

Children's Books

Little Miss Spider by
  David Kirk
Miss Spider's Tea Party
  by David Kirk
The Very Busy Spider by
  Eric Carle

Mary J. Murray, Mazomanie, WI

The Good Deed Caterpillar 4+

LEARNING OBJECTIVES

The children will:
1. Learn to work together.
2. Celebrate the good deeds of their peers.

Materials

images of
    caterpillars
supply of colored
    paper
4" paper circle (for
    a caterpillar
    head)
tape or stapler

VOCABULARY

cooperation   good deeds   kindness   sharing   taking turns

PREPARATION

● Cut paper into 1" × 4" strips.
● Make the circle into a head/face for the caterpillar.

WHAT TO DO

1. Show the children a picture of a caterpillar. Talk to the children about the caterpillar, and ask them to describe how it looks.
2. Explain that you want to make a caterpillar and need the children's help.
3. Each time someone does something kind or helpful for a friend or shares or listens nicely, and so on, that child earns one chain to be put on the caterpillar.
4. Tell the children that you will write down what they did on the strip of paper and attach it to the paper chain to "grow" your caterpillar.
5. Have the children brainstorm actions that might earn them a chain on the caterpillar.

TEACHER-TO-TEACHER TIP

● Encourage the children to notice good deeds that others do in the classroom; keep a pen and paper strips nearby so you can write down the good deeds as they occur.

SONG

● Sing a variation of "If You're Happy and You Know It" with the children, replacing "happy," with words like "share," take turns," and so on.

ASSESSMENT

Consider the following:
● Do the children understand the benefit of doing good deeds and helping one another?
● Can the children think of good deeds that might belong on the good deed caterpillar?

Suzanne Maxymuk, Cherry Hill, NJ

Children's Books

Angelina and the Butterfly by Katherine Holabird
Say Please by Virginia Austin
The Very Hungry Caterpillar by Eric Carle

A Bumblebee Has Stripes 3+

LEARNING OBJECTIVES

The children will:
1. Identify the different characteristics of various bees and wasps.
2. Memorize a song about bumblebees.

Materials

images of different kinds of bees, wasps, hornets

VOCABULARY

bumblebee	honey bee	thin
body	hornet	wasp
hive	stripe	wing

WHAT TO DO

1. Set out the different images of bees, wasps, hornets, and so on.
2. Engage the children in a discussion about the various creatures. Encourage them to describe the visual features of each.
3. Teach the children the following rhyme:

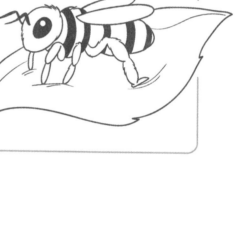

A Bumblebee Has Stripes
by Kristen Peters
A bumblebee has stripes so bold
On yellow bodies I've been told.
With wings that are so paper thin
To help them fly above and in.
They visit flowers, one by one,
Then back to the hive when they are done!

4. Challenge each child to memorize one line of the poem, and have the children recite their lines one at a time, in order.

ASSESSMENT

Consider the following:
- Can the children describe the visual differences between various bees and wasps?
- How well do the children memorize the poem?

Children's Books

The Beautiful Bee Book by Sue Unstead
Bumblebee by Margaret Wise Brown
The Bumblebee Book by Julia Mecham-Rodgers
Ruby Lee the Bumblebee by Dawn Matheson

Kristen Peters, Mattituck, NY

How Insects Move

3+

LEARNING OBJECTIVES

The children will:
1. Describe three ways that insects move: fly, jump, and crawl.
2. Identify at least one insect in each category.

Materials

insect pictures
chart paper

VOCABULARY

ant	beetle	grasshopper
bee	butterfly	wasp

PREPARATION
- Collect pictures of a variety of insects.
- Print poem on chart paper.

WHAT TO DO
1. Gather the children together in a circle.
2. Recite the following poem with the children:

   Itsy, Bitsy Insects by Kathryn Hake
   Some insects fly.
   Some insects jump.
   Some crawl along the ground.
   Some insects buzz.
   Some insects chirp.
   Some never make a sound.

3. Talk with the children about the different ways that creatures move and sound in the poem. Ask the children to identify an insect that performs each action.
4. Show the children images of the various insects throughout this portion of the activity.
5. When the children identify a creature for each action, invite the children to act out that action, saying "Let's pretend we are butterflies and fly around the circle," or "Let's pretend we are grasshoppers and hop from place to place."

ASSESSMENT
Consider the following:
- Pass out pictures. Call each category one at a time. Ask the children to hold up pictures of insects that fly, jump, or crawl.
- Can the children identify the images of individual insects by name?

Children's Books

About Insects:
A Guide for Children by
Cathryn P. Sill
The Very Busy Spider by
Eric Carle
*The Very Clumsy Click
Beetle* by Eric Carle
*The Very Hungry
Caterpillar* by Eric Carle
The Very Lonely Firefly
by Eric Carle
The Very Quiet Cricket
by Eric Carle

Kathryn Hake, Brownsville, OR

How Many Legs?

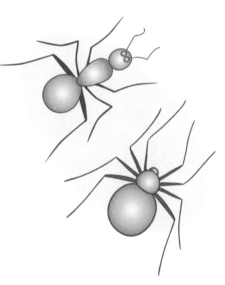

3+

LEARNING OBJECTIVES

The children will:

1. Learn to distinguish between ants and spiders.
2. Learn to count from one to eight.

Materials

VOCABULARY

ant	eight	spider	two
crawl	six	spin	web

WHAT TO DO

1. Ask the children to form a circle and sit down.
2. Sing the following song with the children:

   I Have Two Legs by
   Shyamala Shanmugasundaram
   (Tune: "Are You Sleeping?")
   I have two legs. (raise two fingers)
   I have two legs. (raise two fingers)
   So have you. (turn to the left)
   So have you. (turn to the right)
   Ants have six legs, (raise six fingers)
   Spiders have eight legs, (raise eight fingers)
   Did you know? (turn to the left)
   Did you know? (turn to the right)

TEACHER-TO-TEACHER TIP

- Create spiders by rolling playdough into a ball for the body and adding bendy straws for the legs.

ASSESSMENT

Consider the following:

- Can the children differentiate between an ant and a spider?
- How well do the children act out the fingerplay?

> Shyamala Shanmugasundaram, Nerul, Navi Mumbai, India

Children's Books

Are You an Ant? by
Judy Allen and
Tudor Humphries
Are You a Spider? by
Tudor Humphries
Hey, Little Ant by Philip
and Hannah Hoose
*The Life and Times
of the Ant* by
Charles Micucci
Miss Spider's Tea Party
by David Kirk

Ladybug Poem

3+

LEARNING OBJECTIVES

The children will:
1. Learn about ladybugs.
2. Develop their memorization skills.
3. Recite a poem as a group.
4. Develop their counting skills.

Materials

VOCABULARY

aphid   ladybug   leaf

WHAT TO DO

1. Recite the following poem with the children, holding up the number of fingers indicated throughout:

Ladybug Poem by Cookie Zingarelli
Five little ladybugs sitting on a leaf, eating aphids all day long.
One jumped off and then there were four.
Four little ladybugs sitting on a leaf, eating aphids all day long.
One jumped off and then there were three.
Three little ladybugs sitting on a leaf, eating aphids all day long.
One jumped off and then there were two.
Two little ladybugs sitting on a leaf, eating aphids all day long.
One jumped off and then there was one.
One little ladybug sitting on a leaf, eating aphids all day long.
It jumped off to join the others on another leaf.

TEACHER-TO-TEACHER TIP

- Make ladybug masks by cutting circles from red poster board, cutting holes for eyes and mouth, and letting the children draw black spots. Attach black chenille stems to form antennae. Punch holes on the sides and tie strings to each hole. Help the children put on their masks to act out the poem above.

ASSESSMENT

Consider the following:
- How well do the children recite the poem?
- Are the children beginning to understand the way the number of ladybugs diminishes through the poem?

Children's Books

Are You a Ladybug? by Judy Allen and Tudor Humphries
The Grouchy Ladybug by Eric Carle
Ladybug on the Move by Richard Fowler
Over in the Garden by Jennifer Ward

Cookie Zingarelli, Columbus, OH

The Spider Song

3+

LEARNING OBJECTIVES

The children will:
1. Learn a new song about spiders.
2. Cultivate an interest in rather than fear of spiders.

Materials

pictures of different spiders and their webs
books about spiders (see list for suggestions)

VOCABULARY

alarm   fly   mosquito   poisonous   spider   web

WHAT TO DO

1. Show the children pictures of spiders and talk about how spiders spin sticky webs to catch bugs like flies and mosquitoes.
2. Explain that spiders are very helpful because they eat many bugs we consider pests.
3. Teach the children "The Spider Song." Begin by sitting on the floor with knees drawn up together, hands on knees. Let one hand be the "spider" and place it on your shoe.

The Spider Song by Kay Flowers
(Tune: "Twinkle, Twinkle, Little Star")
There's a spider on my shoe. I don't know just what to do.
Why's the spider on my shoe? Is it stuck there with some glue?
There's a spider on my shoe. I don't know just what to do. (walk spider up to knee)
There's a spider on my knee standing there so quietly.
Why's the spider on my knee? Can't it see that it's on me?
There's a spider on my knee standing there so quietly. (walk spider up onto other arm)
There's a spider on my arm. Maybe I should show alarm.
Why's the spider on my arm? It's not doing any harm.
There's a spider on my arm. Maybe I should show alarm. (shake arms vigorously, and then point to floor)
There's a spider on the floor. Now it's heading out the door.
Why's the spider on the floor? Doesn't it like me anymore?
There's a spider on the floor. Now it's heading out the door. (wave goodbye)

ASSESSMENT

Consider the following:
- Do the children show interest in spider pictures and books?
- Can the children walk hand-spiders over their bodies without fear?

Kay Flowers, Summerfield, OH

Children's Books

Anansi Does the Impossible! An Ashanti Tale retold by Verna Aardema
Little Miss Spider by David Kirk
Miss Spider's Tea Party by David Kirk

The Caterpillar Song

4+

LEARNING OBJECTIVES

The children will:
1. Practice measuring and ordering by length.
2. Develop their understanding of numbers.

VOCABULARY
caterpillar   measure

PREPARATION
- Ahead of time, cut out nine caterpillars in different lengths ranging from 2"–10".
- On the back of each, write the numeral showing how many inches the caterpillar measures.

WHAT TO DO
1. Talk with the children about caterpillars, and how they are different lengths.
2. Teach the children the following song:

    The Caterpillar Song by Susan Oldham Hill
    (Tune: "How Much Is That Doggy in the Window?")
    How much does this caterpillar measure?
    I wonder how long it can be…
    I put it beside my little ruler,
    Now measuring is easy for me!

3. Show the children how to measure correctly by making sure the left end of the ruler is even with the left end of the caterpillar.
4. Tell the children that once they have the edges even on the left, then they should look at the right to see the numeral that is at the right edge. That will tell them how many inches the caterpillar measures. Then they can turn it over to see if they are right.
5. Ask the children to line the caterpillars up in order from shortest to longest.

ASSESSMENT
Consider the following:
- Ask one child at a time to measure caterpillars and to put them all in order by length.
- Can the children count aloud each caterpillar's length in inches?

Susan Oldham Hill, Lakeland, FL

Children's Books

Cause Caterpillar Can in C by Jo Davidson
The Icky Bug Alphabet Book by Jerry Pallotta
I'm a Caterpillar by Jean Marzollo
Inch by Inch by Leo Lionni
The Very Hungry Caterpillar by Eric Carle

Five Little Butterflies

4+

LEARNING OBJECTIVES

The children will:

1. Learn a song about butterflies.
2. Develop their counting skills.

Materials

VOCABULARY

butterfly   five   four   one   three   two

WHAT TO DO

1. Sing the following song with the children:

   Five Little Butterflies by Cookie Zingarelli
   (Tune: "Five Little Chickadees")

   Five little butterflies flying by the door;
   One flew away, and then there were four.

   Chorus:
   Butterfly, butterfly, happy as can be.
   Butterfly, butterfly, fly, fly away.

   Four little butterflies sitting in a tree;
   One flew away and then there were three.

   (Chorus)

   Three little butterflies looking at you;
   One flew away, and then there were two.

   (Chorus)

   Two little butterflies sitting in the sun;
   One flew away, and then there was one.

   (Chorus)

   One little butterfly left all alone;
   It flew away, and then there were none.

2. Challenge the children to reverse the song:

   One little butterfly sitting all alone;
   Along came another and then there were two.

   Butterflies, butterflies, happy and gay;
   Butterflies, butterflies, playing all day.

   Two little butterflies sitting in the sun;
   Along came another and then there were three.

   (Chorus)

   Three little butterflies looking at you;
   Soon came another and then there were four.

   (Chorus)

   Four little butterflies sitting by the door;
   Soon came another and then there were five.

   (Chorus)

ASSESSMENT

Consider the following:

- Are the children able to sing the song together?
- Do the children have any difficulty reversing the song?

Cookie Zingarelli, Columbus, OH

Children's Books

Butterflies by
Emily Neye
Butterfly, Butterfly by
Petr Horacek
*Velma Gratch and the
Way Cool Butterfly* by
Alan Madison
*The Very Hungry
Caterpillar* by Eric Carle

From Caterpillar to Butterfly

4+

LEARNING OBJECTIVES

The children will:
1. Learn about the phases in a butterfly's life.
2. Learn to recite a poem together.

Materials

images of caterpillars, cocoons, and butterflies

VOCABULARY

black	caterpillar	green	moth	yellow
butterfly	cocoon	insect	white	

WHAT TO DO

1. Engage the children in a conversation about caterpillars. Show the children pictures of caterpillars. Ask the children if they know what caterpillars change into.

2. Explain to the children that when they are ready to change, caterpillars make cocoons, and emerge from the cocoons transformed into new creatures. Show the children images of cocoons. Ask the children if they have ever seen a cocoon in nature.

3. Recite the following poem with the children:

Caterpillars by Laura Wynkoop
Caterpillars can be green,
Or yellow, black, and white.
They even come in blue and red,
They're really quite a sight!

4. Show the children images of butterflies. If you have enough images of butterflies, encourage the children to dance around the room waving their images of butterflies around.

ASSESSMENT

Consider the following:
- Can the children describe the phases of a butterfly's life?
- Are the children able to recite the poem together as a group?

Laura Wynkoop, San Dimas, CA

Children's Books

Caterpillar to Butterfly: A Colorful Adventure by Sally Symes
The Crawly Caterpillar by Judith Nicholls
From Caterpillar to Butterfly by Deborah Heiligman
The Very Hungry Caterpillar by Eric Carle

I Can Be an Entomologist 4+

LEARNING OBJECTIVES

The children will:
1. Learn the term "entomologist."
2. Look for insects.

Materials

paper or cardboard
scissors (adult use
    only)
toy insects

VOCABULARY

entomologist   entomology   magnify   magnifying glass   search

PREPARATION

- Cut out magnifying glass shapes from paper or cardboard.
- Set various toy insects out around the classroom.

WHAT TO DO

1. Set out the magnifying glass cutouts, and ask each child to take one.
2. Introduce the children to the word "entomologist" by explaining that entomologists study insects.

3. Teach the children the following song:

   I Can Be an Entomologist by Mary J. Murray
   (Tune: "I'm a Little Tea Pot")
   I'm an entomologist don't you see.
   Bugs are interesting to me.
   I look for insects here and there.
   I study insects everywhere.

4. Invite the children to search around the room for insects while singing the song. When the children find an insect, have them say "I see an insect right here!"
5. Encourage the children to describe the insects they find, and to say the name of the insects if they know them.

ASSESSMENT

Consider the following:
- Do the children understand what an entomologist is?
- Can the children memorize the song?
- Can the children identify the insects they find in the classroom?

Mary J. Murray, Mazomanie, WI

Children's Books

Amazing Bugs by
Miranda MacQuitty
Caterpillars, Bugs,
and Butterflies by
Mel Boring
Monster Bugs by Lucille
Recht Penner

A Spider Weaves

4+

LEARNING OBJECTIVES

The children will:
1. Learn about spiders.
2. Develop their ability to memorize.

Materials

images of spiders

VOCABULARY

spider   trap   weave   web   wrap

WHAT TO DO

1. Engage the children in a discussion about spiders. Show the children images of various spiders.
2. Ask the children where they have seen spiders. Ask the children to talk about how large the spiders were or what they were doing.
3. Explain to the children that spiders live in the webs they make and use the webs to gather food.
4. Teach the children the following poem:

A Spider Weaves by Kristen Peters
A spider weaves to and fro,
A sturdy web she must sew,
Her legs work throughout the day
Hasn't time to rest or play,
Her web's done, no time to sleep,
She awaits for bugs to creep,
A moth flutters in her trap,
Now the moth becomes a wrap,
Hungrily, she eats her meal
One that no one else can steal,
Her great web has fallen apart
Back to the top she must start!

TEACHER-TO-TEACHER TIP

● Challenge the children to come up with physical movements for the different parts of the rhyme.

ASSESSMENT

Consider the following:
● Can the children describe what spiders use their webs for?
● How well do the children recite the rhyme?

Kristen Peters, Mattituck, NY

Children's Books

The Itsy Bitsy Spider by
Iza Trapani
Spiders by
Gail Gibbons
The Very Busy Spider by
Eric Carle

A Very Noisy Mosquito

4+

LEARNING OBJECTIVES

The children will:

1. Explore insect behavior.
2. Communicate personal experiences with insects.

Materials

pictures or transparencies of a bee, mosquito, and fly

VOCABULARY

buzz   drone   fly   mosquito   pesky

PREPARATION

● Hang up or project pictures of the three insects.

WHAT TO DO

1. Walk around the children saying, "Bzzz, bzzz, bzzz!"
2. Once the all the children have heard you, discuss the sounds insects make.
3. Ask if they've ever had a fly or mosquito "bug" them. What were they doing?
4. Why do insects come around people? (food, clothing colors, odors)
5. With the children, act out the following poem:

A Very Noisy Mosquito by Terry Callahan

A very pesky fly
Buzzes around my head. (turn around in a small circle)
I try to make it go away (wave hands around head)
But hit myself instead! (say, "Ow!")

A very noisy mosquito
Hums with a buzzy drone, (hum)
I try to catch it with my hand
(clap hands together)
And it leaves me alone.

A very busy bee stops by
To check me out. (look up and down)
I guess it knows I'm not a flower
(shake head and/or finger "no")
Because it does not hang about.
(wave goodbye)

TEACHER-TO-TEACHER TIP

● Humming can be challenging for some children. If it is challenging for your class to hum, use kazoos instead.

ASSESSMENT

Consider the following:

● Ask the whole class to name an insect you discussed. What does it do?
● Make a worksheet with the three insects on it. Include pictures of a flower, some food, and a person. Ask the children to draw lines from each insect to the picture(s) they feel each connects to (for example, the children could connect the fly to food or a person, the bee to a flower, and the mosquito to a person). Discuss their responses.

Terry Callahan, Easton, MD

Children's Books

Bugs! Bugs! Bugs! by Bob Barner
Flying Insects by Patricia Lantier-Sampon
Why Mosquitoes Buzz in People's Ears by Leo and Diane Dillon

We're Going on a Bug Hunt 4+

LEARNING OBJECTIVES

The children will:
1. Familiarize themselves with insects.
2. Use their observational skills.
3. Learn about the natural world.

Materials

magnifying glasses
empty plastic spice jars
words to the chant
digital camera
paper

VOCABULARY

antennae   bug   hunt   insect   pollinate   pupa

PREPARATION

- Poke holes in the lid of each spice jar.

WHAT TO DO

1. Have the children repeat each line of the following chant after you and move like the insect. Explain that they will move like insects to learn a bit about the insects they are searching for.

   We're Going on a Bug Hunt by Kaethe Lewandowski

We're going on a bug hunt!	*We're going on a bug hunt!*
We're going to catch some big ones.	*We're going to catch some big ones.*
What a sunny day!	*What a sunny day!*
Are you ready? Okay!	*Are you ready? Okay!*
Oh my! A bee!	*Oh, my! An ant!*
A black and yellow bee,	*A tiny, black ant,*
Flying over the flowers.	*Crawling through the grass.*
Buzz, buzz, buzz.	*Shh….*

2. While on the bug hunt, take photos of the process of hunting for the bugs as well as capturing them.
3. Use the magnifying glass to look at the bugs in their natural habitat as well as in the spice jars.
4. Print out the photos you took, and write down what the children tell you about each. Create a class book titled, "Our Bug Hunt."
5. Set the bugs free afterward.

ASSESSMENT

Consider the following:
- Ask the children to describe the bug hunt in the correct sequence.
- Ask the children to describe the differences and similarities in the insects they found on the hunt.
- Ask the children what they see in the printed photos and write down their answers.

Children's Books

Alpha Bugs by David Carter
Bugs by Joan Richards Wright
The Butterfly Hunt by Yoshi
Icky Bug Counting Book by Jerry Pallotta

Kaethe Lewandowski, Centreville, VA

Which One Is It?

4+

LEARNING OBJECTIVES

The children will:

1. Learn a simple way to differentiate between moths and butterflies.
2. Develop their small motor skills.

Materials

pictures of moths and butterflies resting on plants or tree trunks

actual moth and butterfly on plant stems in ventilated jars (optional)

VOCABULARY

antennae   parallel   position

PREPARATION

- Display pictures or jars where the children can readily see them.

WHAT TO DO

1. Hold up pictures of moths and butterflies or jars of actual insects. Note similarities, such as colorful wings and six legs. Point out differences, such as the moth's feathery antennae compared to the butterfly's smooth ones.
2. Explain that the wing position at rest is one of the easiest ways to identify each insect. Butterflies hold their wings parallel and together. (Hold hands up, palms together.) Moths hold their wings flat and side by side. (Hold hands flat, thumbs together.) Teach them the following fingerplay:

Which One Is It? by Kay Flowers
Is it a butterfly? Is it a moth? (thumbs touching, fingers together, flapping like wings)
How can we tell them apart? (shrug shoulders and hold hands out, palms up)
Look at their wings when they are at rest. (point to eyes)
Learn this and you will be smart. (tap head)
Butterfly, (palms together)
Moth, (hands flat)
Butterfly, (palms together)
Moth, (hands flat)
That's how we tell them apart. (hold palms up as if making a point)

3. Release the insects after the children have enjoyed watching them for the day.

TEACHER-TO-TEACHER TIP

- Use the pictures or the actual insects as a math activity. Count wings, antennae, legs, spots, stripes, and so on.

ASSESSMENT

Consider the following:

- Can the children correctly identify resting moths or butterflies?
- Can the children correctly describe wing positions of moths and butterflies?

Children's Books

Butterflies by Karen Shapiro
Butterflies by Emily Neye
Butterfly, Butterfly by Petr Horacek
Velma Gratch and the Way Cool Butterfly by Alan Madison
The Very Hungry Caterpillar by Eric Carle

Kay Flowers, Summerfield, OH

Follow the Ant

3+

LEARNING OBJECTIVES

The children will:

1. Demonstrate ability to wait in line.
2. Demonstrate ability to follow or lead the line.

Materials

VOCABULARY

ants	leader	scent
follow	line	trail

PREPARATION

● Make a line-leader chart, so the children can take turns leading the class (the ants).

WHAT TO DO

1. Call the children to stand in line.
2. Explain that when ants find food, they follow a scent trail from home to the food and back home again. Ants are very quiet.
3. Tell the children that they will now act like ants, following the leader down the trail. At the end of the trail, they will reach their destination (outdoor play, snack area, art stations, and so on).
4. Have the line leader lead the group to this goal.

TEACHER-TO-TEACHER TIP

● If the children are still learning to walk in line, you may need to encourage them as they move from one place to another. Celebrate a job well done by singing "The Ants Go Marching" with the children.

ASSESSMENT

Consider the following:

● Are the children able to wait in line?
● Are the children able to follow the line and lead the line?

Children's Books

The Ants Go Marching edited by Ann Owen
Find Anthony Ant by Lorna and Graham Philpot
Let's Take a Field Trip to an Ant Colony by Kathy Furgang

Sue Bradford Edwards, Florissant, MO

Busy Beehive

4+

LEARNING OBJECTIVES

The children will:
1. Collect and sort toys and blocks.
2. Develop their small and large motor skills.

Materials

recording of the instrumental "The Flight of the Bumblebee" by Nikolai Rimsky-Korsakov
tape player or CD player

VOCABULARY

beehive   buzz   collect   sort   store

PREPARATION

- Read a book about busy bees and their beehive to the class.
- Discuss in simple terms how bees work, going from flower to hive.
- Practice humming or buzzing like a bee.

WHAT TO DO

1. Suggest that the children can be "busy bees" too.
2. Tell the children that they will pretend that the toys and blocks are pollen that they must take back to the hive.
3. Tell the children that they must put their "pollen" in its proper place in the hive.
4. Discuss the proper place for each item in advance.
5. To avoid chaos, give each child a specific "pollen" (blocks, trucks, dolls, and so on) to collect.
6. Play "The Flight of the Bumblebee" and invite the children to buzz around the room until all their pollen is in its proper place.
7. Tell the "bees" where to go (for example, the snack table or to the coat area) after they complete their task.
8. Release the bees in shifts (for example, the "block bees," then the "truck bees," and so on).

FINGERPLAY

Busy, Buzzy Bee by Christina Chilcote
Busy, buzzy bee, (wiggle finger like a flying bee)
1, 2, 3. (show fingers while counting)
Busy, buzzy bee, (wiggle finger like a flying bee)
Stay away from me! (point to self)

ASSESSMENT

Consider the following:
- Do the children understand the vocabulary words?
- Can the children imitate a bee's sound?
- Are the children able to collect their toys and put them away?

Children's Books

Bumblebees by Cheryl Coughlan
Busy, Buzzy Bee by Karen Wallace
I Wonder What It's Like to Be a Bee? by Erin Hovanec
The Beautiful Bee Book by Sue Unstead

Christina Chilcote, New Freedom, PA

Insect Pathway

LEARNING OBJECTIVES

The children will:
1. Learn to follow directions.
2. Identify insects.
3. Practice reading sight words.

Materials

carpet squares (or plastic or fabric placemats)
beanbag toy insects (or large paper insects)
5" × 7" word cards (1 per insect type)
potted plants or artificial plants and flowers
rocks
sticks

VOCABULARY

ant	cricket	fly	inchworm
caterpillar	firefly	grasshopper	ladybug

PREPARATION
- Arrange the carpet squares in the classroom to create a pathway leading from the large group area to the learning centers area.
- Arrange a variety of plants, rocks, and sticks along the pathway to create an outdoor effect.
- Display several beanbag or paper insects along the border of the pathway.
- Display a word card near each insect accordingly.

WHAT TO DO
1. When it's time to transition from one activity to another, invite the children to line up at one end of the pathway.
2. Instruct the children to quietly walk along the insect pathway and identify each insect by name.
3. Remind the children to be careful where they walk so they don't step on any insect friends.
4. Encourage the children to read the word cards as they walk along the trail.
5. When the children reach the opposite end of the pathway they are free to move on to the next activity.
6. Remind the children to walk and talk quietly as they move along the pathway of insects.

ASSESSMENT
Consider the following:
- Walk with the children along the insect pathway and listen as they identify each insect on display.
- Invite individual children to stop and pick up a select insect and then tell their classmates what they know about that specific type of bug.

Children's Books

Bugs! Bugs! Bugs! by Bob Barner
How Many Bugs in a Box? by David Carter
The Very Clumsy Click Beetle by Eric Carle

Mary J. Murray, Mazomanie, WI

Index of Children's Books

A

Aaaarrgghh, Spider! by Lydia Monk, 86

About Insects: A Guide for Children by Cathryn P. Sill, 94

Aesop's Fables by Anna Milbourne, 22

Alpha Bugs by David Carter, 104

Amazing Bugs by Miranda MacQuitty, 84, 101

Anansi Does the Impossible! An Ashanti Tale by Verna Aardema, 11, 26, 34, 97

Angelina and the Butterfly by Katharine Holabird, 56, 92

Ant, Ant, Ant: An Insect Chant by April Pulley Sayre, 16

The Ants Go Marching by Ann Owen, 106

Ants in Your Pants: A Lift-the-Flap Counting Book by Sue Heap, 63

Are There Ants in Your Pants? by Amy Meyer Allen, 63

Are You a Butterfly? by Judy Allen & Tudor Humphries, 14

Are You a Dragonfly? by Judy Allen & Tudor Humphries, 21

Are You a Grasshopper? by Judy Allen, 22

Are You a Ladybug? by Judy Allen & Tudor Humphries, 24, 31, 61, 96

Are You a Spider? by Tudor Humphries, 33, 95

Are You an Ant? by Judy Allen & Tudor Humphries, 12, 27, 95

As Quick as a Cricket by Audrey Wood, 58

B

Barnyard Banter by Denise Fleming, 15

The Beautiful Bee Book by Sue Unstead, 55, 93, 107

The Bee Tree by Patricia Polacco, 50, 67

Beekeepers by Linda Oatman High, 50, 67

The Bee-Man of Orn by Frank R. Stockton, 32, 70, 80, 87

Bees, Bugs, and Beetles by Ronald N. Rood, 37

Bees, Wasps, and Ants by George S. Fichter, 65

Beetle Bop by Denise Fleming, 25, 81

Beetles by Edana Eckart, 25, 81

Beginning Fun with Bugs and Butterflies by Gayle Bittinger, 82

Belinda Bee's Busy Year by Rusty Wise, 50–51, 67

Berlioz the Bear by Jan Brett, 39

The Best Book of Bugs by Claire Llewellyn, 37, 47–49, 69, 71

The Best Bug Parade by Stuart Murphy, 54, 57, 65, 74–75, 78, 84

Big Bugs by Mary Gribbin, 54, 74–75

The Big Honey Hunt by Stan & Jan Berenstain, 88

Billions of Bugs by Haris Petie, 59

Blue Bug's Book of Colors by Virginia Poulet, 40

The Bug Book by William Dugan, 47, 60, 64

The Bug Cemetery by Frances Hill, 10

The Bug Guy: 10 Words by Sean Groathouse, 73

Bug IQ by Roger Priddy, 34

Bug Safari by Bob Barner, 16, 25, 81

The Bugliest Bug by Carol Diggory Shields, 83

Bugs Are Best! by Ruth Thomas, 38, 72, 77

Bugs Are Insects by Anne Rockwell, 77

Bugs by James E. Gerholdt, 82

Bugs by Joan Richards Wright, 104

Bugs by Pat & Frederick McKissack, 59

Bugs! by David Greenberg, 54, 57, 74–75, 78, 84

Bugs Up Close by Diane Swanson, 77

Bugs! Bugs! Bugs! by Bob Barner, 46, 49, 69, 83, 103, 108

The Bumblebee Book by Julia Mecham-Rodgers, 55, 93

Bumblebee by Margaret Wise Brown, 55, 93

Bumblebees by Cheryl Coughlan, 107

Busy, Buzzy Bee by Karen Wallace, 107

Butterflies by Emily Neye, 99, 105

Butterflies by Karen Shapiro, 14, 17–18, 36, 105

Butterflies! by Darlene Freeman, 18

The Butterfly Alphabet by Kjell B. Sandved, 90

Butterfly by Susan Canizares, 14, 17

The Butterfly Counting Book by Jerry Pallotta, 17

Butterfly Express by Jane Belk Moncure, 13, 68

The Butterfly Hunt by Yoshi, 104

A Butterfly Is Born by Melvin Berger, 45

Butterfly, Butterfly by Petr Horacek, 9, 13, 36, 99, 105

Buzz Said the Bee by Wendy Cheyette Lewison, 32, 70, 80, 87

C

The Caterpillar and the Polliwog by Jack Kent, 19

Caterpillar to Butterfly: A Colorful Adventure by Sally Symes, 100

Caterpillars, Bugs, and Butterflies by Mel Boring, 73, 84, 101

Cause Caterpillar Can in C by Jo Davidson, 98

Charlie the Caterpillar by Dom Deluise, 15, 19, 66, 76

Chicka, Chicka, One, Two, Three by Bill Martin Jr. & Michael Sampson, 52

Chirp, Chirp! Crickets in Your Backyard by Nancy Loewen, 79
Clara Caterpillar by Pamela Duncan Edwards, 19, 23, 76
Come See My Bugs by Rozanne Williams, 51
The Crawly Caterpillar by Judith Nicholls, 100
Crickets and Grasshoppers by Ann O. Squire, 22, 43, 79
The Crunching Munching Caterpillar by Sheridan Cain, 23

D
Dazzling Dragonflies: A Life Cycle Story by Linda Glaser, 21
Discovering Crickets and Grasshoppers by Keith Porter, 22, 43
The Dragonfly Next Door by John Adams, 21
The Dragonfly Pool by Eva Ibbotson, 21
Dragonfly's Tale by Kristina Rodanas, 21

E
The Eensy-Weensy Spider by Mary Ann Hoberman &
  Nadine Bernard Westcott, 33

F
Find Anthony Ant by Lorna & Graham Philpot, 106
Fireflies by Julie Brinckloe, 44
Fireflies by Megan E. Bryant, 28
Fireflies in the Night by Judy Hawes, 28, 53
Fireflies, Fireflies Light My Way by Jonathan London, 44
Flying Colors: Butterflies in Your Backyard by Nancy Loewen, 13, 40, 68
Flying Insects by Patricia Lantier-Sampon, 41, 46, 103
From Caterpillar to Butterfly by Deborah Heiligman, 23, 66, 100

G
Good Night Sweet Butterflies by Dawn Bentley, 90
Gotta Go! Gotta Go! by Sam Swope, 57
The Grouchy Ladybug by Eric Carle, 20, 24, 52, 61, 85, 89, 96

H
Have You Seen Bugs? by Joanne Oppenheim, 16, 25, 81
Hey, Little Ant by Philip M. & Hannah Hoose, 12, 27, 95
Hi, Fly Guy by Tedd Arnold, 30
The Honeybee and the Robber by Eric Carle, 20, 32, 39, 51, 70, 80, 87

Honeybee's Busy Day by Richard Fowler, 88
Honeybees by Jane Lecht, 39, 70
How Many Bugs in a Box? by David Carter, 108

I

"I Can't," Said the Ant by Polly Cameron, 27, 63
I Like Bugs by Margaret Wise Brown, 10, 48–49
I Like Bugs: The Sound of B by Alice K. Flanagan, 38
I Love Bugs! by Philemon Sturges, 83
I Wish I Were a Butterfly by James Howe, 45
I Wonder What It's Like to Be a Bee? by Erin Hovanec, 107
I'm a Caterpillar by Jan Marzollo, 98
The Icky Bug Alphabet Book by Jerry Pallotta, 72, 98
The Icky Bug Counting Book by Jerry Pallotta, 104
In the Small, Small Pond by Denise Fleming, 15
In the Tall, Tall Grass by Denise Fleming, 15
Inch by Inch by Leo Lionni, 98
The Itsy Bitsy Spider by Iza Trapani, 33, 62, 86, 102

L

Ladybug on the Move by Richard Fowler, 96
Ladybug, Ladybug by Ruth Brown, 89
Ladybug, Ladybug, Where Are You? by Cyndy Szekeres, 15
A Ladybug's Life by John Himmelman, 24, 61
Ladybugs and Beetles by Sally Morgan, 31
Let's Take a Field Trip to an Ant Colony by Kathy Furgang, 106
The Life and Times of the Ant by Charles Micucci, 12, 27, 95
Little Miss Spider by David Kirk, 11, 26, 33, 86, 91, 97
Look Closer by Brian & Rebecca Wildsmith, 35

M

Manuelo, the Playing Mantis by Don Freeman, 29
Metamorphoses: Butterfly by Arthur John L'Hommedieu, 90
Miss Spider's Tea Party by David Kirk, 11, 26, 35, 42, 47, 60, 91, 95, 97
Monarch Butterfly by Gail Gibbons, 66
A Monarch Butterfly's Life by John Himmelman, 45
Monster Bugs by Lucille Recht Penner, 65, 101
More Bugs in Boxes by David A. Carter, 37, 40, 59–60, 64, 71

My Bug Book by Melissa Steward, 46, 69
My First Book of Bugs and Spiders by Ticktock Media, Ltd., 69
My World: Bees by Christine Butterworth, 88

O

Old Black Fly by Jim Aylesworth, 41, 42
On Beyond Bugs: All About Insects by Tish Rabe, 30, 48
One Hundred Shoes by Charles Ghigna, 78
Oscar and the Cricket by Geoff Waring, 58
Over in the Garden by Jennifer Ward, 96

P

Pattern Bugs by Trudy Harris, 59–60, 64, 71, 78
Praying Mantises by Colleen A. Sexton, 29
Praying Mantises by Jason Cooper, 29
Praying Mantises: Hungry Insect Heroes by Sandra Markle, 29

R

Roberto, the Insect Architect by Nina Laden, 34
Ruby Lee the Bumblebee by Dawn Matheson, 55, 93

S

Sam and the Firefly by P. D. Eastman, 28
Say Please by Virginia Austin, 92
Spiders by Gail Gibbons, 62, 102
Symmetry in Nature by Allyson Valentine Schrier, 90

T

A Taste of Honey by Nancy Elizabeth Wallace, 88
Ten Flashing Fireflies by Philemon Sturges, 28
Ten Little Ladybugs by Melanie Girth & Laura Huliska-Beith, 24, 52, 61, 89
Ten Loopy Caterpillars by Joy Cowley, 56
There Was an Old Lady Who Swallowed a Fly by Pam Adams, 41
Time for Kids: Spiders! by the Editors of Time for Kids, 33, 86

V

Velma Gratch and the Way Cool Butterfly by Alan Madison, 9, 36, 99, 105
The Very Busy Spider by Eric Carle, 20, 26, 31, 62, 85–86, 91, 94, 102

The Very Clumsy Click Beetle by Eric Carle, 10, 20, 25, 48, 94, 108
The Very Hungry Caterpillar by Eric Carle, 9, 13–14, 17–20, 23, 35, 38, 45, 53, 56, 66, 68, 72–73, 76, 85, 92, 94, 98–100, 105
The Very Lonely Firefly by Eric Carle, 20, 42, 44, 82, 94
The Very Quiet Cricket by Eric Carle, 20, 30, 43, 53, 58, 79, 94

W
What About Ladybugs? by Celia Godkin, 53
What's That Sound, Wooly Bear? by Philemon Sturges, 73
Why Butterflies Go by on Silent Wings by Marguerite W. David, 18
Why Mosquitoes Buzz in People's Ears by Leo & Diane Dillan, 103

Index

A

Accountability, 7
Adeney, Anne, 32, 50, 67
Alike/different, 10, 13, 20–21, 28, 30,
    43, 48, 68, 73, 77
Allergies, 32, 50, 88
Ants, 12, 22, 27, 63, 95, 106
Artificial flowers, 67, 108
Asking permission, 49
Assessment
    importance of, 7

B

Balls, 80
    golf, 26
Baskets, 40, 54, 69, 82
Beanbag insects, 37, 54, 64, 82, 108
Beehives, 70, 107
    patterns, 55
Bees, 32, 39, 50, 55, 67, 70, 80,
    87–88, 93, 107
    patterns, 55
    plastic, 67
Bowls, 77, 88–89
Boxes, 40, 57, 59, 80
    checkbook, 59
    large, 58
    shoeboxes, 59, 73
Butterflies, 13–14, 17–18, 21, 23, 36,
    45, 66, 68, 90, 99–100, 105
    plastic, 66
Butterfly nets, 38, 82

C

Callahan, Terry, 103
Cardstock, 42, 45, 101
Carle, Eric, 20
Caterpillars, 13–14, 18–19, 23, 56, 73,
    76, 92, 98, 100
Chart paper, 27, 35, 94
Charting activities, 35, 83

Cheese, 32
    processed, 91
Chenille stems, 13, 73, 96
Chichester, Lisa, 75
Chilcote, Christina, 107
Classification, 16, 85, 94
Clay, 10, 78
Clothespins, 58, 90
Colored pencils, 21, 28–29
Colors, 9, 13, 25, 38, 40, 54, 67–68, 81
Computers, 24, 35
Construction paper, 15, 23, 26, 28, 38,
    52, 59, 61, 74, 85–86
Containers, 80
    plastic, 73
    small, 32, 50, 73
    whipped topping, 40
Cooperative play, 32, 34, 40, 47, 50,
    80, 88, 92
Copy paper box top, 26
Counting activities, 14, 17, 35, 52,
    65, 68, 70–73, 76–78, 81, 83, 85,
    95–96, 98–99, 105
Crayons, 9, 15–19, 21, 23, 29, 33, 60,
    73, 75
Crickets, 43, 58, 79
Cups, 9
    measuring, 88
    paper, 83
    plastic, 31

D

Descriptive language, 54–55, 59, 62,
    66, 68, 74, 77, 103
Dragonflies, 21
Dzierzanowski, Holly, 48

E

Edwards, Sue Bradford, 49, 106
Eye-hand coordination, 47, 86

F

Fabric, 28
    squares, 82
Felt, 13, 65
    eyes, 91
Fermino, Margery Kranyik, 15
Fingerplays
    "Busy, Buzzy Bee" by Christina
        Chilcote, 107
    "The Hungry Caterpillar" by
        Kristen Peters, 23
    "Which One Is It?" by Kay
        Flowers, 105
Fireflies, 28, 44
Five-year-olds
    book activities, 28–29
    games, 52
    language/literacy activities, 29,
        59–62
    math activities, 52, 75–78
    small motor activities, 76, 78
Flowers
    artificial, 67, 108
Flowers, Kay, 36, 87, 97, 105
Fluorescent paint, 28, 44
Following directions, 12, 19, 40, 46, 49,
    63, 65, 67, 81–82, 88–91, 106, 108
Food coloring, 89–90
Four-year-olds
    art activities, 10–12
    book activities, 16–27
    circle time activities, 30–35
    games, 37–51
    language/literacy, 22, 33, 37, 39,
        44, 46, 51, 53–58, 73, 84,
        101, 108
    large motor activities, 38–39, 43,
        45, 49, 64–65, 80, 107
    math activities, 16–17, 35, 65,
        70–74, 84–85, 98–99, 105

    music/movement activity, 79
    outdoor play, 16, 80, 104
    sand/water play, 83
    science/nature activities, 84–85
    small motor, 10–12, 17–19, 23,
        25–26, 34, 47, 54, 58, 71, 79,
        83, 87, 89–90, 105, 107
    snack/cooking activities, 89–91
    social/emotional development,
        92
    songs/poems/fingerplays,
        98–105
    transition activities, 50,
        107–108
Fruits
    apples, 88
    dried, 91

G

Games
    Birthday Bug Bags, 37
    Bugs on the Rug, 38
    Buzzin' Bees, 39
    Capture a Bug, 40
    Catch a Fly, 41
    Crickets and Grasshoppers, 43
    Fireflies, 44
    Flutter-Hop, 36
    Fly Like a Butterfly, 45
    Freeze Dance, 44
    Insect Cards, 46
    Insect Dominoes, 47
    Ladybug Counting Game, 52
    Match the Insects, 48
    Meet My Flying Friend, 42
    Mother, May I Move Like an
        Insect? 49
    Smell Out Your Group! 50
    Where's That Bug? 51
Glitter, 11, 18, 62

Glue, 11, 15, 18–20, 31, 56, 60, 62, 72, 74, 76, 87
    sticks, 24, 39, 42, 45, 52–53, 59, 66, 85
    tacky, 12
Graham crackers, 91
    crumbs, 88
Grasshoppers, 22, 36, 43

H
Hake, Kathryn, 94
Hammond, Janet, 16, 19, 80
Hill, Susan Oldham, 53, 72, 98
Hole punches, 62, 86, 96
Huffstetler, Erin, 9
Hutmacher, Kimberly, 12

I
Index cards, 25, 30, 52–53, 61
Insect-identification handbooks, 84
Insects
    beanbag, 37, 54, 64, 82, 108
    stuffed, 37

L
Ladybugs, 24, 61, 89, 96
    patterns, 61
Laminate, 23, 24, 46–47, 57, 70, 77
Left-to-right movement, 30
Length, 73, 98
Letter knowledge, 38, 53, 55, 58, 61–62
Lewandowski, Kaethe, 26, 104
Life cycles
    butterflies, 13–14, 18–19, 23, 100
    dragonflies, 21
    ladybugs, 24
Listening skills, 22, 36, 41, 59–60
Lucas, Eileen, 77

M
Magazines, 20, 24, 59, 77
Magnifying glasses, 84, 104
Markers, 11, 13, 15, 18–19, 23–24, 27, 30, 35, 38–39, 42, 45, 47, 52–53, 60, 70
    permanent, 25, 58, 67
Masking tape, 36, 51, 64, 86
Matching activities, 47–49, 52–53, 55, 57–58, 66, 72
Maxymuk, Suzanne, 51, 56, 92
Measuring activities, 16, 73, 75, 88–89, 98
Memory skills, 23, 48, 51, 82, 93, 96, 102
Metamorphosis, 13–14, 18–19, 23, 100
Milk
    cartons, 87
    powdered, 88
Mitchell, Patrick, 10, 34, 41, 46, 57, 78
Moran, Jane, 89
Mural paper, 15, 68
Murray, Mary J., 13, 30–31, 37–38, 40, 43, 54, 59, 64–65, 68, 73, 81–82, 84, 91, 101, 108

O
Observation skills, 16, 21, 43, 51, 57, 104
One-to-one correspondence, 47, 70

P
Paint, 58
    face, 14
    finger paint, 25
    fluorescent, 28, 44
    pens, 61
    tempera, 26

Paper, 11, 16–17, 19–21, 29, 33, 55, 60–61, 75–76, 92, 101, 104
  cardstock, 42, 45, 101
  chart, 27, 35, 94
  construction, 15, 23, 26, 28, 38, 52, 59, 61, 74, 85–85
  contact, 59
  mural, 15, 68
  poster board, 18, 51, 96
  tissue, 37, 68, 72, 90
  wax, 9, 11–12, 25, 32, 44, 50, 58
Paper cups, 83
Paper cutouts, 17, 31, 51, 64, 66, 75, 108
Paper fasteners, 60–61
Paper plates, 15, 56, 62, 68, 86, 91
Paste, 15, 20
Patterns, 9, 55, 71
Peanut butter, 32, 50, 88
  jars, 54
Pencils, 11, 13, 16, 29, 60, 73
  colored, 21, 28–29
Pens
  correction fluid, 61
  felt-tip, 76
  paint, 61
Permanent markers, 25, 58, 67
Peters, Kristen, 23, 25, 44, 55, 58, 61–62, 71, 90, 93, 102
Phonemic awareness, 39, 45, 53, 58
Pictures, 9–10, 12, 16, 21, 24, 27, 30, 33, 35–37, 39–40, 42–43, 45–47, 53, 56–58, 60, 68, 71, 73–78, 84–85, 87, 91–94, 97, 100, 102–103, 105
Pipe cleaners, 18, 58, 72, 90
Plants
  stems, 105
  potted, 108
Plastic
  animals, 85
    bees, 67
    bins, 73, 84
    bottles, 81
    butterflies, 66
    containers, 73
    cups, 31
    grass, 58
    insects, 31, 37, 69, 81, 84–85, 101
    jars, 54, 104
    spiders, 86
    spines, 24
    tubs, 68
Pocket charts, 35, 70
Poems
  "Bloomin' Bugs" by Laura Wynkoop, 69
  "A Bumblebee Has Stripes" by Kristen Peters, 93
  "Caterpillars" by Laura Wynkoop, 100
  "Five Little Flowers" by Cookie Zingarelli, 88
  "Here Is a Beehive," 67
  "Holding the Light" by Kristen Peters, 44
  "Itsy, Bitsy Insects" by Kathryn Hake, 94
  "Ladybug Poem" by Cookie Zingarelli, 96
  "Ladybug" by Kristen Peters, 61
  "Little Miss Muffet," 34
  "Little Spider" by Shirley Anne Ramaley, 33
  "Meet My Friend," 42
  "Quick Little Insect" by Kristen Peters, 71
  "A Spider Weaves" by Kristen Peters, 102
  "A Very Noisy Mosquito" by Terry Callahan, 103

"We're Going on a Bug Hunt" by Kaethe Lewandowski, 104
Pollination, 80, 87, 107
Pompoms, 18, 67
Popsicle sticks, 44, 79
Positional words, 44, 51
Poster board, 18, 51, 96
Puzzles, 57, 76

R
Raisins, 90–91
Ramaley, Shirley Anne, 21, 29, 33
Recipes
    butterfly snacks, 90
    honey milk balls, 88
    ladybug cookies, 89
    spider web snacks, 91
Recorded music, 44
    "Firefly" by Nancy Stewart, 44
    "The Flight of the Bumblebee" by Nikolai Rimsky-Korsakov, 107
Rhyming activities, 27, 33–34, 42, 44, 56, 61, 67, 69, 71, 88, 93–94, 96, 100, 102–104
Romig, Hilary, 52, 74
Rubber bands, 32, 50, 65
Rulers, 16, 73, 98
Ryan, Sandra, 86

S
Scissors, 13, 17–18, 20, 23–24, 38–39, 45, 47, 50, 52, 55, 57, 59, 61, 65–66, 68, 70–71, 72, 74, 86–87, 98, 101
Sensory activities, 32, 41, 50, 84
Sequencing skills, 24, 61, 76, 104
Shanmugasundaram, Shyamala, 14, 95
Shapes, 13, 19, 38, 74, 90
Sharkey, Susan, 20, 22, 28, 63, 83
Shaughnessy, Monica, 79

Shoeboxes, 59, 73
Shoes, 71
    baby, 71
Singing activities, 14, 23, 25–26, 48, 51, 54, 58, 64, 77, 82, 90, 92, 95, 97–99, 101, 106
Sizes, 13, 68, 72–73
Snacks
    butterfly, 90
    honey milk balls, 88
    spider web, 91
Social/emotional skills, 31–32, 37, 47, 50, 59, 64
Socks, 40, 65
Songs
    "The Ants Go Marching," 48, 51, 63, 77, 106
    "Butterfly Wings" by Kristen Peters, 90
    "The Caterpillar Song" by Susan Oldham Hill, 98
    "Five Little Butterflies" by Cookie Zingarelli, 99
    "The Hungry Caterpillar" by Kristen Peters, 23
    "I Can Be an Entomologist" by Mary J. Murray, 101
    "I Have Two Legs" by Shyamala Shanmugasundaram, 95
    "I'm a Little Beetle" by Kristen Peters, 25
    "I'm a Little Cricket" by Kristen Peters, 58
    "I'm Walking with My Bug" by Mary J. Murray, 64
    "If You're Happy and You Know It," 92
    "Spider Song," 26
    "The Spider Song" by Kay Flowers, 97

"Ten Little Butterflies," 48

"Ten Little Butterflies" by Shyamala Shanmugasundaram, 14

"Twinkle, Twinkle, Little Bug" by Mary J. Murray, 82

"What's Inside This Jar?" by Mary J. Murray, 54

Sorting activities, 16, 37, 68–69, 72, 85, 107

Spider webs, 11, 26, 34, 41, 62, 86, 91, 97, 102

Spiders, 26, 33–34, 41, 62, 86, 91, 95, 97, 102
    plastic, 86
    rings, 62
    stamps, 26

Spoons
    measuring, 89
    wooden, 89

Staplers, 60, 62, 92

Stickers, 31, 37, 47–48, 61, 81

String, 18, 61, 71, 96

Styrofoam
    balls, 18
    blocks, 67

Sugar, 89
    powered, 89

T

Tagboard, 24, 35, 39, 47, 70, 81, 98

Taking turns, 43, 47, 82

Tape, 11, 75, 92
    masking, 36, 51, 64, 86

Three-year-olds
    art activity, 9
    book activities, 13–15

    game, 36
    language/literacy activities, 15, 82
    large motor activities, 15, 36, 63
    manipulatives activities, 66–67
    math activities, 14, 68–69, 81, 95–96
    rest time activities, 81–82
    small motor, 9, 67, 69, 86
    snack/cooking activity, 88
    songs/poems/fingerplays, 93–97
    transition activities, 36, 106

Tissue paper, 37, 68, 72, 90

Tongs, 26, 67

Tracing, 62, 70

Troy, Terry, 27

V

Ventilated jars, 36, 105

Verbal clues, 63

Vilardi, Debbie, 85

Vinegar, 32, 50

W

Wax paper, 9, 11–12, 25, 32, 44, 50, 58

Word cards, 84, 108

Wright, Jackie, 24, 35, 39, 42, 45, 47, 60, 66, 70

Wynkoop, Laura, 69, 100

Z

Zingarelli, Cookie, 11, 17–18, 76, 88, 96, 99

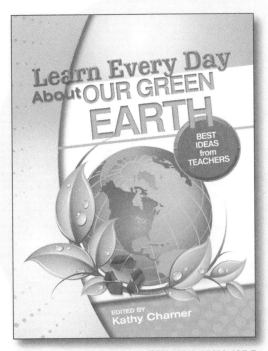

ISBN 978-0-87659-127-7
Gryphon House / 12015 / PB

ISBN 978-0-87659-126-0
Gryphon House / 11001 / PB

Learn Every Day About COLORS
100 BEST IDEAS from TEACHERS
EDITED BY Kathy Charner

ISBN 978-0-87659-088-1
Gryphon House / 13467 / PB

Learn Every Day About NUMBERS
100 BEST IDEAS from TEACHERS
EDITED BY Kathy Charner

ISBN 978-0-87659-090-4
Gryphon House / 15573 / PB

Learn Every Day About SHAPES
100 BEST IDEAS from TEACHERS
EDITED BY Kathy Charner

ISBN 978-0-87659-092-8
Gryphon House / 16247 / PB

The Encyclopedia of **Infant and Toddler Activities**

For Children Birth to 3

Written by Teachers for Teachers

Edited by Kathy Charner, Maureen Murphy, and Charlie Clark

ISBN 978-0-87659-013-3
Gryphon House / 13614 / PB

The **GIANT** Encyclopedia of Preschool Activities for **Three-Year-Olds**

Over 600 Activities Created by Teachers for Teachers

Edited by Kathy Charner and Maureen Murphy

ISBN 978-0-87659-237-3
Gryphon House / 13963 / PB

The **GIANT** Encyclopedia of Preschool Activities for **Four-Year-Olds**

Over 600 Activities Created by Teachers for Teachers

Edited by Kathy Charner and Maureen Murphy

ISBN 978-0-87659-238-0
Gryphon House / 14964 / PB

The **GIANT** Encyclopedia of **Kindergarten Activities**

Over 600 Activities Created by Teachers for Teachers

Edited by Kathy Charner, Maureen Murphy, and Jennifer Ford

ISBN 978-0-87659-285-4
Gryphon House / 18595 / PB

The **GIANT** Encyclopedia of **Lesson Plans**
For Children 3 to 6

More Than 250 Lesson Plans Created by Teachers for Teachers

Edited by Kathy Charner, Maureen Murphy, and Charlie Clark

ISBN 978-0-87659-068-3
Gryphon House / 18345 / PB

the **GIANT** encyclopedia of theme activities for children 2 to 5

Over 600 Favorite Activities Created by Teachers for Teachers

ISBN 978-0-87659-166-6
Gryphon House / 19216 / PB

The **GIANT** Encyclopedia of **Monthly Activities**
For Children 3 to 6

Written by Teachers for Teachers

Edited by Kathy Charner, Maureen Murphy, and Charlie Clark

ISBN 978-0-87659-012-6
Gryphon House / 15002 / PB

The **GIANT** Encyclopedia of **Transition Activities**
for children 3 to 6

Over 600 Activities Created by Teachers for Teachers

Edited by Kathy Charner, Maureen Murphy, and Charlie Clark

ISBN 978-0-87659-003-4
Gryphon House / 12635 / PB

ISBN 978-0-87659-001-0
Gryphon House / 11325 / PB

ISBN 978-0-87659-181-9
Gryphon House / 16413 / PB

ISBN 978-0-87659-044-7
Gryphon House / 16948 / PB

ISBN 978-0-87659-193-2
Gryphon House / 18325 / PB

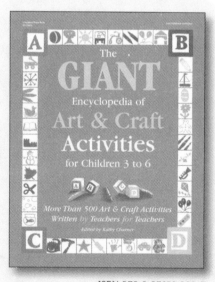

ISBN 978-0-87659-209-0
Gryphon House / 16854 / PB